Stitch 'n Flip
QUILTS

14 FANTASTIC PROJECTS

Valori Wells

C&T PUBLISHING

Copyright © 2000 Valori Wells

Editor: Annie Nelson
Technical Editor: Joyce Engels Lytle
Copyeditor: Steven Cook
Cover & Book Designer/Design Director: Christina Jarumay
Graphic Illustrations: Kari Jane Santos © C&T Publishing, Inc.
Production Coordinator: Kathy Lee
Production Assistant: Claudia Boehm
Photography: Valori Wells
Front Cover: *Johnny Jump-ups* by Valori Wells

Attention Teachers:
C&T Publishing, Inc. encourages you to use this book as a text for teaching. Contact us at 800-284-1114 or www.ctpub.com for more information about the C&T Teachers Program.

We take great care to ensure that the information included in this book is accurate and presented in good faith, but no warranty is provided nor results guaranteed. Since we have no control over the choice of materials or procedures used, neither the author nor C&T Publishing, Inc. shall have any liability to any person or entity with respect to any loss or damage caused directly or indirectly by the information contained in this book.

Library of Congress Cataloging-in-Publication Data
Wells, Valori.
Stitch 'n flip quilts : 14 fantastic projects / Valori Wells.
     p. cm.
Includes index.
ISBN 1-57120-111-4 (pbk.)
 1. Patchwork--Patterns. 2. Quilting--Patterns. 3. Patchwork quilts.
I. Title: Stitch and flip quilts. II. Title.
TT835 .W4785 2000
746.46'041--dc21

00-008188

Trademarked (™) and Registered Trademarked (®) names are used throughout this book. Rather than use the symbols with every occurrence of a trademark and registered trademark name, we have only used the symbol the first time the product appears. We are using the names only in an editorial fashion and to the benefit of the owner, with no intention of infringement.

Published by C&T Publishing, Inc.
P.O. Box 1456
Lafayette, California 94549

Printed in China
10 9 8 7 6 5 4 3 2 1

Table of Contents

Dedication

This book is dedicated to two wonderful women in my life.

To my mom, Jean Wells, for everything: her unconditional love and support, her nurturing of my creative spirit, her faith in me, her calm words when I was frustrated, and most of all her friendship. Thanks, Mom—I love you.

To my dear friend, Connie McFarlene, for teaching me to love every moment, to live in the now, and to cherish life. Through her love of life and sense of humor, I am a better person. Thanks, Connie— I love you.

Acknowledgements

I wish to acknowledge the following people who have made *Stitch 'n Flip* such a fabulous book.

Thanks to: Barb, Mary, Lawry, Barbara, and Mom for contributing their beautiful quilts and encouraging words to this book.

Todd Hensley and the C&T family for believing in me and giving me a chance to create this book.

Annie Nelson for her great job as my developmental editor. She helped me find my words at times.

Joyce Lytle, my technical editor, for her patience, for understanding of all my questions and requests, and for seeing the light at the end of my schematics.

Christina Jarumay, who designed the beautiful, fresh, artistic layout of *Stitch 'n Flip*. Thank you for giving my book the extra splash of personality that makes it unique.

Kathy Lee and Diane Pedersen for their efforts as my production coordinators; Kari Santos, my illustrator; Claudia Boehm for all her scanning and efforts as my production assistant.

Warner and Beth, Mary and Lewis, and Janet for letting me photograph my quilts on their property.

John, my wonderful step-dad, for all the humor and love he brought to the "sewing factory."

And finally, The Stitchin' Post girls for all of their support and critique of my work. I treasure all of them and their love.

Introduction

I had just graduated from college in 1997 when I visited my mother to take a mini-quilting lesson. Within this lesson, she taught me how to make a Stitch 'n Flip block using a strip-piecing method on a muslin foundation. I fell in love with this technique, as I could see exploring it in many directions; the possibilities seemed endless. My first quilt using the Stitch 'n Flip technique was *Memories of My Mother's Garden*, shown in *Through the Garden Gate*, co-authored with my mother Jean Wells. I found Stitch 'n Flip to be fun and appropriate for my ambitious quilting ideas. As a beginning quilter, I was pleased to find a technique that accommodated my ideas without being complicated.

I asked several friends to each contribute a project to this book. Out of all of the contributors, Mom and I were the only ones who had previously tried the Stitch 'n Flip technique. I gave everyone a mini-lesson similar to the instructions within the *Johnny-Jump-Ups* project in Chapter 1 (page 7). From there, each created a design of her own. I was amazed to see how the designs and fabric selections within the quilts reflected the style and personality of the makers. Each of them expressed how the Stitch 'n Flip technique is simple and forgiving, giving dramatic results without being difficult.

In *Stitch 'n Flip Quilts: 14 Fantastic Projects*, you will find projects to fit any level of quilting expertise or style. Included are Stitch 'n Flip designs based on traditional blocks, such as *Vintage Fans* (page 73) and *Forever in Blue Jeans* (page 81), as well as contemporary flower designs, as shown in *Johnny-Jump-Ups* (page 7) and *Anniversary Bouquet* (page 57). You can also use Stitch 'n Flip to create frames for your memories and treasured moments, as shown in *A Dozen Windows* (page 32). Mary, a beginner quilter, quickly picked up this technique and has decided it's a favorite. She made decorative pillows (page 37) and a table runner (page 65), and is now planning a quilt. The final quilt, *Cathedral Falls* (page 88), explores Barb Tate's creative process—a journey that started at a special place on a river and progressed to the design wall. I hope this chapter inspires you to explore Stitch 'n Flip as a design process.

Chapter 1 introduces the basic Stitch 'n Flip method. Each chapter that follows explores Stitch 'n Flip variations and explains how the projects are quilted. Fabric selection is also covered for each quilt, which will help you make decisions when choosing fabrics for your projects. Watch for "Tips," which alert you to helpful hints and techniques. I hope you enjoy your Stitch 'n Flip quilting journey!

Stitch 'n Flip

CHAPTER 1

Basics

Stitch 'n Flip is a simple process you can use as a launching pad for a variety of designs, as you will see on the following pages. Once you've determined your design, use a foundation fabric as the base for piecing. Cut the foundation fabric 1/2" larger, to allow for 1/4" seam allowances. All of the following projects use a muslin foundation, but other stable, lightweight fabrics will also work. However, a paper foundation does not work as well. The seams can become distorted when you tear away the paper foundation.

1 On your foundation, place a fabric shape close to the center. As you can see from the variety of projects in this book, it can be as simple as a triangle or as complex as an eight-sided shape.

2 The widths of the strips of fabric are cut based on each project's instructions.

3 Add the strips around the raw edges of the shape, stitching, flipping, and finger-pressing until the muslin foundation is covered. Press. Square up the block, trimming excess fabric to the size of the foundation piece.

You can create a variety of shapes, including fans, stars, flowers, and diamonds, depending on how the strips are added. Detailed instructions accompany each project.

I have included patterns, drawings, and photographs of quilting designs for your personal use and inspiration. Enlarge any of these designs to your desired size using a photocopy machine. All of the machine quilting that I do is free-motion quilting. The term "free motion" refers to using a darning foot and dropping the feed dogs on your sewing machine, which allows you to move your quilt randomly through the machine and control your stitch length. I use a clear darning/embroidery foot because it allows me to see the stitching on the surface of the quilt as it progresses. Aim for a stitch length that is neither too close together nor too far apart. To accomplish this, keep a steady, generous amount of pressure on the foot pedal as you maneuver your quilt through the machine. I practice free-motion quilting with a 20"-square fabric sandwich (fabric, batting, fabric). Your practice-square needs to be large enough so you can move it around freely and sense how it feels when the feed dogs aren't controlling the fabric. You can mark quilting designs freehand on the quilt, or use templates, using a marker that washes out. It's that easy. Once you develop a rhythm with the movement of the quilt under the needle and the speed of the pedal, you'll find endless possibilities with free-motion quilting. It just takes practice.

For finishing instructions, refer to your favorite basic quilting books. (For recommendations, see Sources, page 93.) All of the binding yardage requirements are based on 2 1/4"-wide strips cut for double-fold bindings. The *Johnny-Jump-Ups* quilt kicks off this exciting quilt design technique. I know you will enjoy the results.

Johnny-Jump-Ups

L ast fall, Johnny-Jump-Ups were planted in the windowbox outside of my office. Every morning when I went to work, their little smiling faces made my day more enjoyable. When the first snow arrived, I rushed to work thinking they would be dead. Much to my surprise, there they were, surrounded by melting snow in the winter sunlight. In the spring and early summer, they are some of the first flowers to appear in the garden and are often found in mountain meadows.

Johnny-Jump-Ups by Valori Wells, 39 1/2" x 33 1/2", 1999.

Fabric Selection

When pansy fabric came into the store last spring, my idea of a Johnny-Jump-Ups quilt became a reality. Using photographs and the pansy fabric as a guide, I started collecting purples, yellows, and greens. Meadow-style prints work well for the background, since Johnny-Jump-Ups also grow in the wilderness. I cut the flower centers from the pansy print, then took hints as to color placement from the flowers themselves. I used a dark green for the appliqué leaves.

Johnny-Jump-Ups *fabric palette*

Materials

Muslin: 3/4 yard
Purples: Eight to ten, 1/8 yard each for flower blocks
Yellows: Three to four, 1/8 yard each for flower blocks
Small pansy print: 1/8 yard for centers and flower and foliage blocks
Greens: Seven to eight, 1/8 yard each for flower background and foliage blocks. One of the prints is a transition fabric, which has larger pansies and some green foliage. Transition fabrics form a bridge between color groups within a design.
Dark green: 1/4 yard for leaves
Border inset: 1/4 yard
Inner border: 3/8 yard
Outer border and binding: 3/4 yard
Backing: 1 1/4 yards
Batting: 37" x 43"

Cutting

Muslin: Cut thirteen 6 1/2" squares (**A**), sixteen 3 1/2" squares (**C**), and six 3 1/2" x 6 1/2" rectangles (**B**).
Flower fabrics: Cut one 1"-wide strip and one 1 1/2"-wide strip.
Foliage fabrics: Cut one 2 1/2"-wide strip.
(Cut more strips of the above flower and foliage fabrics as needed.)
Border inset: Cut sides 1" x 24 1/2"; cut top and bottom 1" x 30 1/2".
Inner border: Cut sides 2" x 24 1/2"; cut top and bottom 2" x 33 1/2".
Outer border: Cut sides 3 1/2" x 27 1/2"; cut top and bottom 3 1/2" x 39 1/2".

Block Construction

Flowers

1. Patterns are provided for the small and large flower centers (page 14). Cut shapes from the fabric you want to be in the centers of the flowers; I used the small pansy print for most of the centers. After cutting a few flowers, you may find that you can cut them freehand. Remember, whatever shape you start with in the center determines the finished shape.

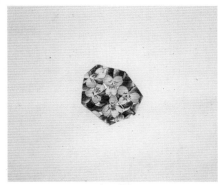

Start the flower

2. Start with a 6 1/2" muslin foundation square. Place the flower center fabric near the center of the muslin. Pin in place.

3. It doesn't matter which side of the flower center you begin on. Place a narrow strip, right sides together, on top of one of the edges of the center. Stitch through the two layers of fabric and the muslin. Flip over the strip and finger-press. Trim the end even with the lines of the sides next to it.

Stitch strip

Trim strip

4. Continue adding strips. Stitch, flip, finger-press, and trim until you have surrounded the center of the flower. (This is reminiscent of how a Log Cabin block is made, by surrounding the center square with strips.) As you add strips, you can use the same fabric or change fabrics, depending on how you want the flower to look.

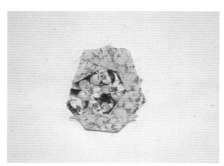

Add strips around the center

The next round

5. Continue adding strips in a circular fashion until the flower is as large as desired.

Finished flower

6. Add the background strips in the same manner until the muslin foundation is completely covered. Because they are wider, they will create a wedge-like effect when added around the flower. Press. Be sure to use some transition fabrics, such as ones that include colors from the meadow and pansy fabrics. Transition fabrics help guide the eye around the quilt and integrate all the colors.

Add foliage to the flower block

7. Square up the block, trimming it to the original cut size of the muslin block's measurement.

8. Complete the remainder of the flower blocks as indicated in the quilt assembly diagram, page 12.

Foliage

1. To make a foliage block, cut a wedge-shaped strip and place it near the center of the muslin.

Foliage block

2. Place a strip on one side of the wedge with right sides together. Stitch and flip. Finger-press. As you proceed, you can angle the strips to create wedges. Add strips lengthwise to the block to create flower stems. Stitch and flip, then press. Trim each piece to make large triangles. On the other side of the center wedge, add a strip. Stitch and flip, then press. Trim each side to create a large triangle shape.

Stitch strip   *Stems of flowers*

3. Use transition fabric throughout the piecing process to visually tie the colors together. Adding transition fabrics as wedges makes the stems more distinguishable.

Transition fabric

> **Tip** *To add interest to the block, place the center of the flower toward one side of the muslin so that the flower is at one end or corner of the block. Add foliage to complete the flower block.*

4. Continue adding strips until you've covered the muslin foundation. Press. Square up the block, trimming excess fabric to the unfinished block size.

Finish foliage block

5. Complete the remainder of the foliage blocks.

Quilt Assembly

1. Arrange the blocks, following the quilt assembly diagram. First stitch smaller units together into sections, then stitch the sections together in the numbered seam order. For seams 3 and 4, stitch from corner to edge, backstitching at the beginning of the seam.

2. Fold the inset strips in half lengthwise, wrong sides together, and press. Pin to the top of the quilt, matching raw edges and overlapping the edges in the corners.

Inset border

3. Add the inner side borders on top of the inset and stitch the seams. The inset stays between the two layers and acts as an accent in the design. Press the seam toward the border. Add the top and bottom borders in the same manner.

4. Add the outer side borders, then the top and bottom borders. Press the seams toward the outer border.

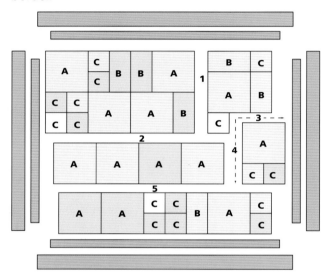

Quilt assembly

Measurements given in cut sizes:
A= 6 1/2" x 6 1/2"   **B**= 3 1/2" x 6 1/2"
C= 3 1/2" x 3 1/2"

Needleturn Appliqué

Add needleturn appliqué leaves where they look visually pleasing. I appliquéd 19 leaves on my quilt.

1. Using a washable marking pencil, trace the two leaf shapes onto the right side of the fabric. Cut them out, adding 3/16" seam allowance. Pin each leaf in place using small straight pins.

Tip *To make the leaves easier to needleturn, finger-press the seam allowance under on the marked line.*

2. Begin on one of the sides. I like to use a milliners #10 needle and thread that matches the fabric. Needleturn under approximately 1/2" to 1" length of fabric at a time along the fold line.

3. From the wrong side of the background fabric, bring the needle up through the folded edge of the leaf, catching only a couple of threads. Bring the needle back down through the background fabric right beside where the previous stitch was taken. Carry the thread along the back approximately 1/8" before you bring it up again.

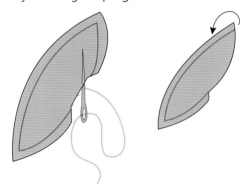

4. To make a point, stitch to the point of the pencil line. Take the tip of the needle and pull the seam allowance around and under. Continue stitching.

Quilting

I made a copy of a pansy using a photocopy machine, then traced the shape to make a template. Using free-motion quilting, I quilted pansy shapes in the centers of the flowers and leaf shapes in the foliage areas. I repeated the pansy shape in the border.

Johnny-Jump-Ups *quilting designs*

Johnny-Jump-Ups Patterns

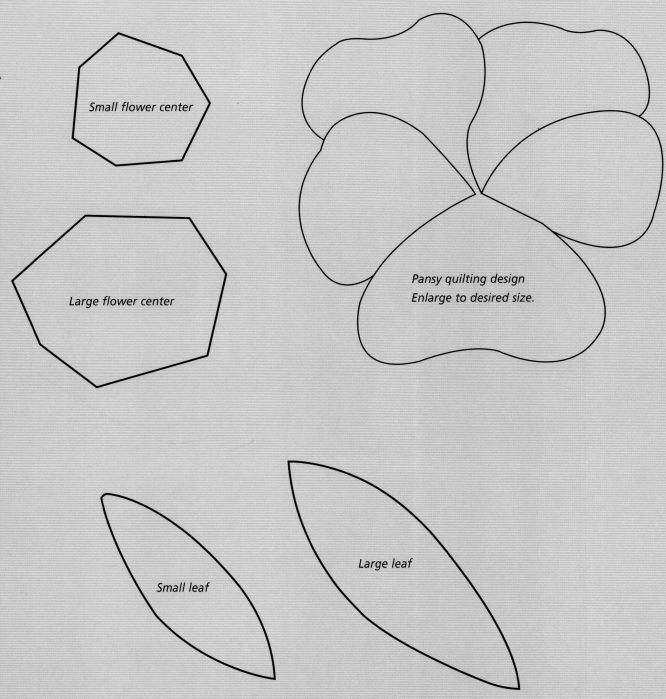

Small flower center

Large flower center

Pansy quilting design
Enlarge to desired size.

Small leaf

Large leaf

Add 3/16" seam allowance to outside edges of leaves.

Color
Symphony

This quilt was made for my dear friend Jen—a vibrant and loving person I know from college. I wanted to make a bold, colorful quilt for her and knew that Stitch 'n Flip was the perfect technique to use with a new design. The name, *Jennabug*, comes from Jen's nickname when she was growing up, and it seemed to fit this bright, fun quilt. I used diamonds as the basic block shapes because of the way they fit together. Choosing just a few colors for Jen wasn't easy, so I decided to use all of the colors on color wheel.

Jennabug by Valori Wells, 82 ¹/₂" x 90 ¹/₂", 1999.

Fabric Selection

Color plays a major role in the designing and making of quilts. I use the color wheel as an inspirational tool. Red, yellow, and blue are primary colors. If you're painting with red, yellow, and blue, you can create every color possible. Look at the color wheel and see how it works. *Jennabug* depicts the color wheel in fabric.

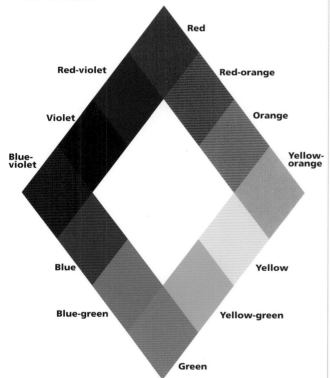

I began with yellow for a couple of reasons. First, yellow doesn't have as much of a variety within its hue as the other colors on the wheel. Second, because it's the lightest color I used, I wanted to make sure that it was contained within the other colors. I made some sketches with colored pencils on paper to get a feel for how the design was going to look. The yellow reminds me of the sun and the other colors radiate from it. From yellow, *Jennabug* graduates to orange and then to red. The red moves into a fuchsia, or red-violet, and then into violet. There is more violet in the quilt than any other color; however, if you were to start with a color other than yellow, you would not want to use as much violet. Violet, opposite from yellow on the color wheel, is yellow's complementary color. I approached using the blues and the greens within the quilt a little differently. I moved the blue into turquoise, to blue-green, to lime green, and finally into a deep forest green. If the quilt continued from the green back to yellow, I would have used the lime green last because of how yellow it is. Since I was using green as the last color, I felt it needed to be darker to contain the quilt and act as a border.

When choosing your fabric, select a variety of colors that move from pale to bright. This creates interesting movement within the blocks. It's helpful to keep a color wheel handy when you're choosing fabric for this quilt. If you already have a fabric stash, you've got a great start. Use as many fabrics as you want, as this quilt is very scrappy. The *Jennabug* design can easily be adapted to any color palette.

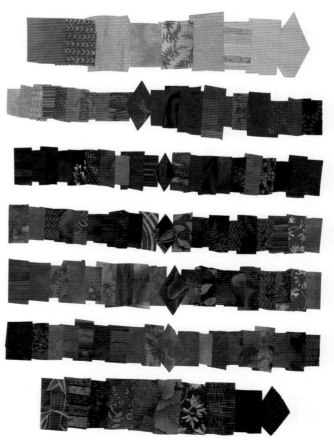

Jennabug *colors arranged by individual diamond palettes*

Materials

Muslin: 5 1/2 yards

For each color group listed, choose fabrics from pale to bright (refer to color palettes on page 17).

Total yardage for each color group:

Yellows: 2/3 yard

Oranges: 1 1/8 yards

Reds: 5/8 yard

Violets: 2 3/4 yards

Blues: 3 1/8 yards

Turquoises: 2 1/8 yards

Yellow-greens: 2 yards

Blue-greens: 3/4 yard

Dark greens: 3 2/3 yards total: 1 3/8 yards for blocks, 1 5/8 yards for borders, 2/3 yard for binding

Backing: 6 yards

Batting: 86" x 94"

Template plastic

Cutting

Make a full diamond template using the quarter-diamond pattern on page 26. The finished size of each diamond is 12" wide x 20" high.

Cut 39 full diamonds from the muslin.

Using the same pattern, make a horizontal half-diamond template, a vertical-half diamond template, and a corner quarter-diamond template using the following guidelines:

Cut 10 horizontal half-diamonds from the muslin.

Add 1/4" seam allowance to the horizontal side.

Cut 6 vertical half-diamonds from the muslin.

Add 1/4" seam allowance to the vertical side.

Cut 4 quarter-diamonds from the muslin.

Add 1/4" seam allowance to the horizontal and vertical sides.

To make centers for the full diamonds, cut rectangles, approximately 3" x 5", and trim each into a diamond shape. Cut the following:

1 yellow

8 red

14 violet

8 blue

4 blue-green

4 yellow-green

To make centers for the horizontal half-diamonds, cut rectangles, approximately 3" x 4", then trim each into half-diamonds. Cut the following:

6 blue-green

4 yellow-green

To make centers for the vertical half-diamonds, cut rectangles, approximately 2 1/2" x 5", then trim each into half-diamonds. Cut the following:

6 dark green

Cut the remaining fabric into 1"-wide and 1 1/4"-wide strips.

Cut fifty 5 1/2" x 7" rectangles out of dark greens for the border.

Block Construction

1. Your centers are diamonds. You will always be working with a diamond or half-diamond shape. For general Stitch 'n Flip instructions, refer to Chapter 1 (page 6).

2. Place the diamond center on your piece of muslin, close to the middle. It does not need to be exact.

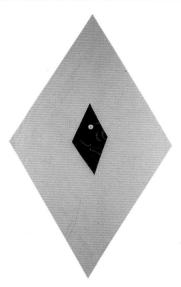

Start the block

3. Set your color palette beside you as you piece. Stitch one round at a time, moving through your palette until the muslin is covered with fabric. Piece in the same order and direction around the block for each color. Trim excess fabric using your template.

Blocks in progress

4. Make one entirely yellow block (**A**).

Yellow block

5. Make two blocks with red centers (**B**), split horizontally: 1/2 orange to yellow, 1/2 red to fuchsia.

Yellow to red, split horizontally

6. Make two blocks with red centers (**C**), split vertically: 1/2 orange to yellow, 1/2 red to fuchsia.

Yellow to red, split vertically

7. Make four blocks with red centers (**D**): 3/4 orange to yellow, 1/4 red to fuchsia.

3/4 yellow and 1/4 red

8. Make four blocks with violet centers (**E**), split horizontally: 1/2 blue, 1/2 violet to fuchsia.

Violet to blue, split horizontally

9. Make two blocks with violet centers (**F**), split vertically: 1/2 blue, 1/2 violet to fuchsia.

Violet to blue, split vertically

10. Make eight blocks with violet centers (**G**): 3/4 violet to fuchsia, 1/4 blue.

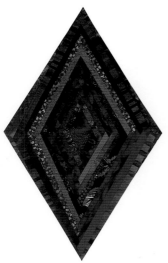

3/4 violet and 1/4 blue

11. Make eight blocks with blue centers (**H**): 3/4 blue, 1/4 turquoise.

3/4 blue and 1/4 turquoise

12. Make four blocks with blue-green centers (**I**), split vertically: 1/2 turquoise, 1/2 yellow-green.

Turquoise and yellow-green, split vertically

13. Make four blocks with yellow-green centers (**J**), split vertically: 1/2 blue-green, 1/2 yellow-green.

Blue-green and yellow-green to dark green, split vertically

14. Make six horizontal half-diamonds with blue-green centers (**K**). Complete the rest of the block with turquoise.

Turquoise half-diamond, split horizontally

15. Make four horizontal half-diamonds with yellow-green centers (**L**). Complete the rest of the block with yellow-green.

Yellow-green half-diamond, split horizontally

16. Make six vertical half-diamonds with dark green centers (**M**). Complete the rest of the block with green.

Dark green half-diamond, split vertically

17. Make four quarter-diamonds, use dark green strips for the center (**N**). Complete the rest of the block with green.

Dark green quarter-diamond

Quilt Assembly

1. Stitch the blocks together into diagonal rows. Press seams of alternate rows in opposite directions.

2. Stitch the rows together. Press seams.

> **Tip** *When stitching the blocks together, you may find that you have large, bulky seams that don't lie in one direction. The best thing to do is simply steam and press seams open with an iron. This also makes it easier when quilting through layers.*

3. Stitch the dark green 5 1/2" x 7" border pieces together, short end to short end, into one long strip.

4. Cut two strips 72 1/2" long for top and bottom borders. Stitch onto quilt. Press.

5. Cut two strips 90 1/2" long for the side borders. Stitch onto quilt. Press.

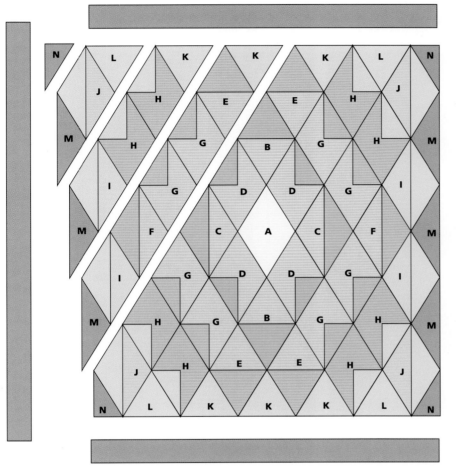

Quilt assembly

Quilting

I started in the center of the quilt with a sun design that radiates toward the orange fabric. I quilted flowers in the space around the red and purple fabrics. To fill-in around the flowers, I added a continuous swirl pattern. Then I quilted more flowers and again filled in with the swirl pattern. For the outer green areas and the border, I quilted leaves and vines. The quilting patterns are on page 25.

Jennabug *quilting designs*

Jennabug Quilting Designs

Enlarge to desired size.

Sun

Flower

Continuous swirl

Leaves and vine

Quarter-Diamond Pattern

Rotate template plastic to trace other half or whole diamond shapes.

Add $1/4$" seam allowance to vertical or horizontal edge of half-diamonds.

Framing
CHAPTER 3
Techniques

This little lavender quilt is a quick and fun project featuring one of my favorite herbs. I love lavender and wanted to use some of its buds in the quilt along with the photos. I created a little pouch for the dried lavender so I could enjoy the fragrance. You can put photos of a loved one in place of the lavender photos and a small treasure in the pouch. There are endless possibilities for this quilt, and it makes a great gift for someone special.

Lavender

Lavender by Valori Wells, 18" x 30", 1999.

Fabric Selection

When choosing fabric, I took hints from observing lavender plants and studying photographs. Think about the role you want the fabric to play with your photographs. What colors are important to make your quilt coherent? I chose greens and purples with lots of movement in their prints to resemble the plant. To keep the focus on the photographs and treasure pouch, I framed them using a hand-dyed fabric.

Materials

Muslin: 1/2 yard

Photo transfers or theme fabric: Two 3" x 6"

A handful of lavender or small treasures

Netting or tulle: 3" x 4" piece

Light lavender: 1/8 yard for treasure pouch

Dark purple: 1/8 yard for photo sashing

Variety of purples: 1/2 yard

Variety of greens: 1 yard

Sashing and border: 1/4 yard purple

Binding: 1/4 yard dark purple

Backing: 2/3 yard

Batting: 22" x 34"

Cutting

Muslin: Cut two rectangles, one 17" x 15" and one 9" x 15".

Light lavender for treasure block:
Cut one 4" x 5" piece.
Cut one 2" x 22" strip for the first round.

Dark purple for photo block:
Cut one 1 1/2" x 6" strip for the center sash.
Cut one 1 3/4"-wide strip, then cut the strip into two 8 1/2" lengths for the side sashing and two 6 1/2" lengths for the top and bottom sashing.

Purple for sashing and border:
Cut one 2" x 15" strip for the sashing between the photos and the treasure block.
Cut two 2" x 15" strips for the top and bottom borders. Cut two 2" x 30" strips for the side borders.

Purples and greens for piecing: Cut 2"-wide strips.

Backing: 22" x 34"

Block Construction

1. Refer to page 36 for photo transfer instructions.

2. The block centers are the sashed photos and the treasure pouch. You will add strips around these elements. For general Stitch 'n Flip instructions, refer to Chapter 1 (page 6).

3. Stitch a photo to each 6" side of the 1 1/2" x 6" dark purple sashing strip. Press toward the sashing.

4. Stitch the 1 3/4" x 6 1/2" sashing strips to the top and bottom of the photos. Press toward the sashing.

5. Stitch the 1 3/4" x 8 1/2" sashing strips to the sides of the photos. Press toward the sashing.

6. On the 17" x 15" muslin rectangle, place the photos (with sashing) 3 1/4" from the top and centered within the 15" width.

7. Add strips of purple and green to fill the muslin.

8. When the muslin is covered with fabric, press and trim to 17" x 15".

9. Stitch three sides of the 3" x 4" netting or tulle onto the 4" x 5" piece of lavender fabric. Place the lavender or treasures into the pouch. Stitch the remaining side.

10. On the 9" x 15" muslin rectangle, place the treasure pouch 2 1/2" from the top and centered within the 15" width.

11. Use the 2" x 22" light lavender strip for the first round around the treasure pouch.

12. Add strips of purple and green to fill the muslin.

13. When the muslin is covered with fabric, press and trim to 9" x 15".

Quilt Assembly

1. Stitch the 2" x 15" purple sashing strip to the bottom of the photo block and to the top of the treasure pouch block. Press toward the sashing.

2. Add the 2" x 15" top and bottom border strips. Press toward the border.

3. Add the 2" x 30" side border strips. Press toward the border.

Lavender *quilting design*

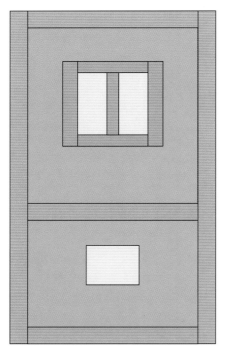

Quilt assembly

Quilting

I stitched-in-the-ditch around the photos and treasure pouch. I then echoed the lavender's plant structure within the Stitch 'n Flip part of the quilt, keeping the stitching lines vertical to mimic the feeling of growth.

Lavender *quilting design*
Enlarge to desired size.

Buttonhole Stitch

1. Thread a needle with two strands of embroidery floss. Bring the needle up from the back of the fabric along the edge of the netting or tulle.

2. Hold the thread with your left thumb (reverse for left-handed stitchers). Take a stitch, inserting the needle into the netting or tulle toward the outside edge ("inside out" is a good reminder). The needle travels over the thread your left thumb is holding. Pull the stitch into place until the thread along the edge is secure and slightly taut.

3. Hold the working thread with your left thumb and take another stitch. When you come to a corner, take a stitch into the corner.

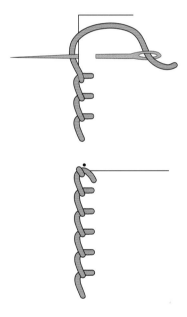

 To add more interest to the treasure pouch, outline it using a buttonhole stitch 1/2" from the edge.

Decorative Running Stitch

I used a decorative running stitch with two strands of floss beyond the buttonhole-stitched edge of the lavender pouch. The key to making this stitch decorative is to make larger stitches on the top surface and smaller stitches underneath.

A Dozen Windows

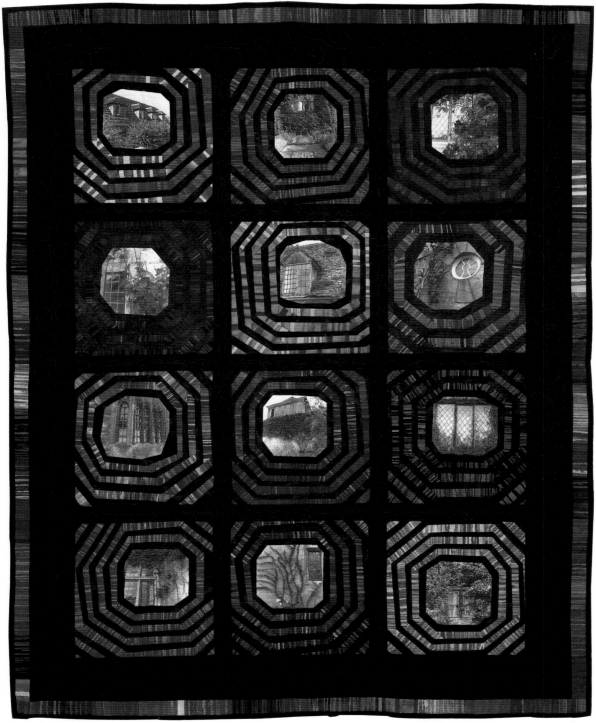

A Dozen Windows by Valori Wells, 37 ½" x 47 ½", 1999.

I created the blocks in *A Dozen Windows* using a photo transfer technique. In May of 1999, my mom and I traveled to England to do some photography for an upcoming book. We spent time exploring the countryside, which is filled with quaint villages. As we traveled, my camera was always at hand; I was constantly shooting photos. When I picked up my film from the developer, I found that I had photographed many windows and doors, especially while we were in the Cotswolds. I decided to transfer them to fabric and make a quilt. One of the most important things to me when working with a photo transfer project is ensuring that the photos remain the focus of the quilt. To make the black and white photographs more interesting, I added a little color to them with fabric markers. For photo transfer instructions, refer to page 36.

Fabric Selection

I have a collection of batik stripes in my fabric stash and decided that they would complement my window idea. I found that alternating black fabric with striped fabric keeps the focus on the photos. Using a different colored stripe for each block to make the quilt more interesting, I arranged the blocks so that their individual colors guide the eye around the quilt.

Materials

Muslin: 1 1/8 yards
Twelve 5 1/2" square photo transfers:
(I used windows, but you could use photos of family members, a vacation, pets, flowers, etc.)
Stripes: Twelve different, 1/4 yard of each for blocks and outer border
Black: 2 yards for blocks, sashing, inner border, and binding
Backing: 1 1/2 yards
Batting: 41" x 51"

Cutting

Muslin: Cut twelve 9 1/2" squares.
Black: Cut twenty-seven 1"-wide strips for blocks.
Stripes: Cut three 1"-wide strips from each.
Sashing: Cut five 1 1/2"-wide strips, cut into seventeen 9 1/2" lengths and six 1 1/2" squares for corner posts.
Inner border: Cut two 3 1/2" x 29 1/2" strips for top and bottom borders. Cut two 3 1/2"-wide strips and a 3 1/2" x 9 1/2" rectangle. Stitch together end to end, then cut into two 45 1/2" strips for the side borders.
Outer border: Cut two to three 1 1/2" x 6 1/2" strips from the twelve different stripes. Choose a pleasing arrangement and stitch together end to end. Cut into two 37 1/2" strips for top and bottom borders. Cut into two 45 1/2" strips for side borders.

Block Construction

1. To maintain the focus on the photos, keep the blocks simple. Start at the corner of each photo and trim around the image until it has eight sides. They will not all look the same. For general Stitch 'n Flip instructions, refer to Chapter 1 (page 6).

2. Place the photo on your muslin foundation, slightly off-center.

3. Start with the black strips for the first round. The black fabric frames the image.

4. Once the black round is done, choose a colored stripe. You don't have to start at the same place. Starting at a different place for each round creates more interesting blocks.

5. Continue alternating each stripe round with a black round. Because the image isn't in the center, you will come to the edge of the muslin on some rounds before you do the rest of the block. Just remember to continue alternating the two colors until you cover the muslin.

6. Press the blocks and square up to 9 1/2".

Quilt Assembly

1. Arrange the blocks and add the sashing strips vertically between them. Press toward the sashing.

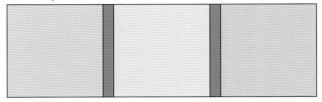

2. Make three horizontal sashing rows as shown. Press toward the sashing strips.

3. Join the block and sashing rows together. Press toward the sashing rows.

4. Add the top and bottom inner borders. Press toward the border. Then add the side borders. Press toward the border.

5. Add the side outer borders. Press toward the border. Then add the top and bottom borders. Press toward the border.

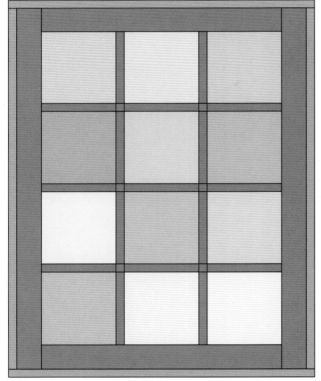

Quilt Assembly

Quilting

I quilted a continuous vine and leaf design in the sashing (page 35). To mimic my designs, start at the bottom right, with the vine and leaf on the right side of the sashing. When you reach the top of the block, pivot and quilt along the horizontal sashing, continuing back to the vertical sashing. Continue up the quilt again and repeat at the next horizontal sashing. Once at the top, quilt the same design back down the quilt, pivoting at the mid-center of the horizontal sashing. Repeat for the left side of the quilt.

For the border, I quilted a similar vine and leaf design in a larger scale. Starting at the bottom middle, quilt around and up to the top middle, continuing back down to where you started. Repeat on the other side. I didn't machine quilt the photo transfers because I felt that it would distract from the image, so I added a bit of hand quilting instead. I simply outlined a few aspects of the photo, such as a leaf or part of a building. Hand quilting secures the three layers and adds detail.

Start here

Leaves and vine quilting designs
Enlarge to desired size.

A Dozen Windows *quilting designs*

Photo Transfer

There are numerous ways to transfer your photographs to fabric. Following is the technique that I like. I use a Hewlett Packard® 140 color copier to transfer photos onto Cannon Fabric Sheets®. Then I remove the acetate backing and wash the photocopy in cold water with Synthrapol®. Washing the sheets in Synthrapol makes the images permanent. Next, I rinse them and iron them dry. It is best to iron on the wrong side of the photocopy to ensure "setting," although air drying sets images as well. For *A Dozen Windows* (page 32), I added color to my black and white photos using fabric markers. I found that a little color goes a long way to create visually-appealing photos. Adding color to the foliage and other areas of the buildings creates detail and interest in simple black-and-white photos. For more techniques, ideas, and information for transferring photographs to fabric, refer to Sources (page 93).

Pillows

Pillows by Mary Ferguson, each 18" x 18", 1999.

When I asked Mary, a new quilter, if she would like to make something for this book, she said she was interested in learning a new technique, but she was a little nervous that she wouldn't be able to do it. Well, she picked it up quickly and was excited about how easy it was. These pillows demonstrate how you can use motifs in fabric to create interesting Stitch 'n Flip blocks.

Fabric Selection

Choose a theme or motif fabric, preferably a design that is big enough to see clearly on a pillow. Select a couple of colors from your chosen motif fabric that you want to pull out and use for the Stitch 'n Flip construction. Use one of these fabrics as an accent color, as this will make your pillow or quilt sparkle. Notice how the black and brown fabrics, used to separate the fabric selections, can be quite striking.

Materials

Muslin: 1/2 yard

Motif fabric: 1/3 yard of fabric to cut out the center motif for the pillows. (We used a fabric that had at least a 3" motif.)

For the butterfly pillow:
  Black: 1/3 yard (includes border fabric)
  Blue: 1/4 yard
  Yellow accent: 1/8 yard

For the leaf pillow:
  Brown: 1/3 yard
  Green: 1/4 yard
  Black accent: 1/8 yard (includes border fabric)

Backing: 1/3 yard

18" pillow form or pillow stuffing

Cutting

Muslin: Cut one 16 1/2" square for one pillow.

Center motif: Cut an approximate 8 1/2" x 9 1/2" piece.

Piecing: Cut fabrics into 2"-wide strips.

Accent piecing: Cut fabric into 1 1/2"-wide strips.

Border: Cut two 1 1/2" x 16 1/2" pieces for the sides, cut two 1 1/2" x 18 1/2" for the top and bottom from the black strips.

Backing (if using a pillow form): Cut two 18 1/2" x 11" pieces.

Backing (if stuffing the pillow): Cut one 18 1/2" square.

Block Construction

1. Cut out your motif into a desired shape, remembering that your cut shape determines how your finished block will look. Mary chose to cut an irregular shape. Be creative—you'll like the results. Make sure you leave at least 1/4" seam allowance around the image. For general Stitch 'n Flip instructions, refer to Chapter 1 (page 6).

2. Place your motif on the muslin. For one of her pillows, Mary placed the motif just off-center. With the other, she placed the motif to the top right. Placement of the motif causes different effects.

3. Mary chose to angle some of her strips to create interesting designs within the pillow. Even though the strips are 2", you can angle them when you're stitching on a strip. Trim excess seam allowance.

4. Alternate different colors of fabric for every round.

5. Use the accent color only a couple of times.

6. Once you cover the muslin with strips, press and trim to 16 1/2" square.

7. Stitch the 1 1/2" x 16 1/2" strips onto the sides of the pillow top for a narrow border. Press toward the border. Stitch the 1 1/2" x 18 1/2" strips onto the top and bottom of the pillow top. Press toward the border.

8. If you are stuffing your pillow, skip to Step 12.

9. For the backing pieces, press a 1/4" hem on the 18 1/2" edge. The 11" side will now measure 10 3/4". Fold down 1/4" again, hiding the raw edge, and stitch near the edge.

10. Place the pieced pillow top and the backing pieces right sides together, lining up the outside edges. The 1/4" seam that you just created should overlap in the middle of the pillow top. Pin the outside edges and stitch around the whole pillow using a 1/4" seam allowance. Trim excess fabric on each corner.

11. Turn the pillow right side out and insert a pillow form.

12. For stuffing, you'll need your back to be a 18 1/2" square.

13. Place the pieced pillow top and the backing right sides together and pin the edges.

14. Stitch 1/4" seam around the whole pillow leaving at least a 3" opening. Turn it right side out and stuff it with pillow stuffing.

15. Hand stitch the 3" opening closed.

Monochromatic
CHAPTER 4
Color Study

Moon Phases was inspired by the moon block that I made for my quilt *Memories of My Mother's Garden*, shown in *Through the Garden Gate*. I wanted to create a quilt using one color group and thought that a moon design lent itself to this concept. To create movement throughout the quilt, I split many of the moon blocks in half. As I split the blocks and stitched them back together, the design took on a life of its own. Each block is different from the next.

Moon Phases

Moon Phases by Valori Wells, 62 ½" x 74", 1999.

Fabric Selection

I started with the lightest gray that I could find and moved through all shades of the color to black. It's important to use a wide variety of prints and textures so that the quilt remains visually interesting. Using prints with black, white, and gray gives the impression of stars shimmering in the night sky. The moon block can be interpreted in a variety of colors, which would dramatically change the look of the quilt. Think about how this quilt would look in a palette of blues! Playing with color is a fun and important aspect of creating quilts.

Fabric selection

Materials

Muslin: 2 3/4 yards
Collect a palette of fabrics in each of the following color groups:
Black to medium-dark gray: 2 2/3 yards for the sky
Light gray to medium-light gray: 2 2/3 yards for the moons
Medium gray: 1/4 yard (I only used a small amount of medium gray in the quilt because I wanted there to be contrast between the moon and sky)
Inner border: 1/2 yard light gray
Outer border: 1/2 yard each of four of your darkest blacks
Binding: 1/2 yard
Backing: 3 3/4 yards
Batting: 66" x 77"

Cutting

Muslin: Cut eight 12" blocks, twelve 13" blocks, and three 6 1/2" x 12" blocks.

Moon fabrics: Cut a 1"-wide and 1 1/2"-wide strip from each fabric.
Sky fabrics: Cut a 1 1/2"-wide and 2"-wide strip. Cut more strips from all the fabrics as you need them.
Inner border: Cut six 2 1/2"-wide strips. Stitch end to end into one long piece. Cut into 58" long for the sides and 50 1/2" long for the top and bottom.
Outer border: Stack the four black fabrics and cut two 6 1/2"-wide strips from each. Leave the strips stacked and cut the following lengths: two 5 1/2", two 7 1/2", and one 9 1/2". Mix these up and stitch into one long strip end to end. Cut into the following: (**A**) 62 1/2", (**B**) 50 1/2", (**C**) 22", (**D**) 41", (**E**) 29", and (**F**) 10 1/2". Refer to the quilt assembly diagram (page 43) for the piecing arrangement.

Block Construction

1. The construction of this block is very similar to the Johnny-Jump-Up block (page 7). Because you are working in a circle, the strips for the moon shape are narrower in order to keep the moon round. For general Stitch 'n Flip instructions, refer to Chapter 1 (page 6).

2. Cut a 3" square from light gray fabric. To create the moon center, trim the square until it has seven or eight sides and is fairly round. Your moon blocks will be more interesting if the centers are not all cut the same way. When placing your center shapes on the muslin, it's important to place them off-center. For the half-moon blocks, you can create interesting splits by moving the center to a different place on the muslin. Remember to leave enough room for some background.

Center shape on muslin

3. Start piecing with narrower strips and work toward wider ones on the outside of your center shape.

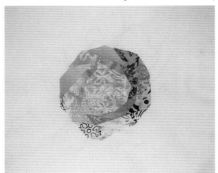

Piecing around the moon

4. As you enlarge the moons, you may find it necessary to make additional angular cuts to your strips to keep the moon circular. Do this by cutting the outside edge of the strip at an angle. I find that cutting this way only works when you cut the angle back to the edge of the previous strips you attached. It's important that the edge of the fabric that will have a strip attached is cut at the same angle as the piece already there.

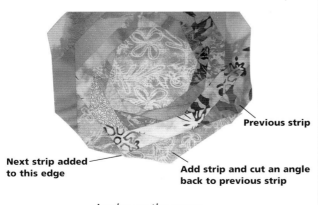

Previous strip

Next strip added to this edge

Add strip and cut an angle back to previous strip

Angles on the moon

5. When you become satisfied with each moon's shape and size, start adding sky fabrics. It's easiest to start with your narrowest strips.

Add sky fabric

6. Once you have covered the muslin foundation, iron the blocks and trim to the original muslin block size. The 13" blocks are your half-moon blocks. They need to be cut on the diagonal and then mixed with each other and sewn back together. You may find after they are sewn back together that the block is larger than 12". You will need to trim it down to 12" square.

Full moon block

Split moon block

Quilt Assembly

1. Once you've completed your blocks, sew them together in horizontal rows. I arranged them so that the full-moon blocks were mixed with the split-moon blocks. Some of my split moons came out more dramatically than others. I find that the split moons add movement to the quilt.

2. Add the 58"-long inner border to the sides of the quilt. Then add the top and bottom 50 1/2"-long light-gray borders. Press toward border.

3. The three 6 1/2" x 12" moon blocks are for the outer border.

4. Referring to the quilt assembly diagram, piece the bottom border and each side. Add the top (B) and bottom (F/moon/E) borders to the quilt top. Then add the side borders (A/moon and D/moon/C) to the quilt top. Press toward outer border.

Quilting

I quilted simple curves in a random pattern mimicking the moon shapes.

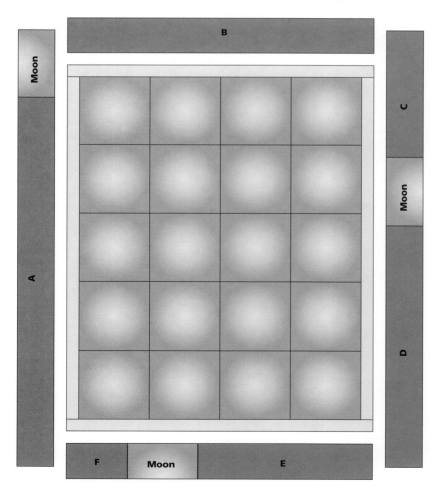

Moon Phases *quilting designs*

Placemats and Centerpiece

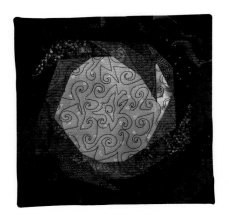

Placemats and *Centerpiece* by Valori Wells, each 16" x 16".

I've always admired a table set with interesting placemats. They make any occasion special and festive. These placemats are easy to make and complement any table. I wanted each of them to be unique, so I made them square instead of rectangular, and I colored each one differently. You can make just one, if you like, and use it as a table centerpiece. This is a fun and easy project that makes a perfect gift.

Fabric Selection

I thought it would be nice to use one color group per placemat but still have them coordinate. If you use a placemat as a centerpiece, you can coordinate your settings or tablecloth to match and create a beautiful table. For each color group, I started with light in the center and graduated outward to dark. Of course, this order can be reversed. The design is fairly simple, so the quilting shows nicely.

Color palettes

Materials

Muslin: 1 yard

Lights, mediums, and darks: 3/4 yard total of each color group. (Make sure you have a light that is at least 8" x 8" for the center.)

Backing: 1 yard

Batting: 1 yard (optional). I used Quilters Dream Cotton™; weight: Request Cotton (the thinnest loft)

YLI Jeans Stitch® thread: Color to match each color group

Cutting

Muslin: Cut three 16 1/2" squares.

Light: Cut one 8" square of each color group for the center.

Light, medium and dark of each color: Cut 2 1/2"-wide strips.

Backing: Cut three 16 1/2" squares.

Construction

1. The placemats start with a center similar to the Johnny-Jump-Up block (page 7), only larger. For general Stitch 'n Flip instructions, refer to Chapter 1 (page 6).

2. Trim the 8" center square until it has seven or eight sides. Place it in the center of the muslin and pin to keep it from slipping while stitching.

3. Start with the lights for your first round. After attaching each strip, trim (the strip only) into a triangle.

4. Use the medium colors for the second round and part of the third round, gradually moving into the darks. Continue trimming strips into a triangle with each addition.

5. Fill the rest of the muslin with darks.

6. Press. Trim your block to 16 1/2" square.

Assembly

Layer as you would a pillow, right sides together, with batting on top. I used a thin cotton batting for the inside; however, batting is optional. Stitch around the placemat, leaving an opening large enough to turn the placemat right side out. Trim the corners, turn right side out, and press. Blind stitch the opening closed.

Quilting

I used a heavy thread (YLI Jeans Stitch) for emphasis. I quilted each one differently to make them individual —as are the people who sit at your dinner table.

Placemats *and* Centerpiece *quilting designs*

Placemats and Centerpiece Quilting Designs

Enlarge to desired size.

Designing from Nature

*A*utumn Aspen was inspired by my stepfather. Last fall, he made a trip over the mountains and came home enamored by the glorious colors of the fall leaves. He said, "I have a quilt idea for you." The aspens were just beginning to change here in Oregon as I started designing this quilt. I watched the aspens change from lime green to bright yellow, and from gold to orange. As I observed the trees, I noticed blue sky peaking through the changing leaves. I took a few photos of the changing trees for reference.

Autumn Aspen

Autumn Aspen by Valori Wells, 57 ½" x 78 ½", 1999.

Fabric Selection

I took my fabric cues from the trees themselves. I didn't want to limit my palette to only gold and orange; combining the colors of the trees' progression seemed more interesting. I made sure that there was a variety of values within each color group. It's also important to use some transition fabrics. A transition fabric guides your eye from an orange to gold by having both colors in it. I continued introducing these as I progressed from one color to the next. As the trees lost their leaves, the silhouettes of the trees became exposed and powerful. I looked for a simple fabric that would mimic aspen bark. The border is very important in this quilt, as it needs to contain all of the elements. I chose the deepest color that I saw on the aspen tree to create an intense, rich border.

Fabric palette

Materials

(**Note:** *Enlarge pattern to 47" x 68", or approximately 800%.*)

Muslin: 3 1/2 yards

Tree leaves:
   Oranges: 3/4 yard
   Golds: 1 1/4 yards
   Yellows: 3/4 yard
   Yellow-greens: 1/2 yard

Note: *Make sure that within your fabric selection you have transition fabrics that tie orange to gold, gold to yellow, and yellow to yellow-green.*

Blues: 3/4 yard

Tree trunk: 1 1/2 yards

Border: Approximately 1/4 yard each of 8 to 10 darker oranges and rusts.

Backing: 3 1/3 yards

Binding: 5/8 yard or use leftover scraps

Batting: 60" x 81"

Template plastic

Freezer paper

Cutting

Muslin: See Step 2 of Block Construction.

Tree leaves and trunk: Cut fabric into 1 1/2"-wide and 2"-wide strips.

Border fabrics: Using the patterns on page 56, make two templates using template plastic. Cut out 29 large and 29 small trapezoid shapes.

Block Construction

1. Enlarge the drawing on page 55 to 47" x 68" using a photocopy machine. Large sections have to be taped together to make the full-size quilt. (You could easily reduce the size of this quilt.)

2. It's easier to cut out a section at a time of the enlarged pattern. Start with a section between the branches. Trace and label each pattern piece in a section onto freezer paper, adding 1/4" seam allowance on all sides. Iron the freezer-paper pattern onto the muslin and cut out the shape. Remove the freezer-paper pattern and Stitch 'n Flip the muslin.

3. Always start with a triangle on your foundation. Every time a strip is added, trim the strip to a triangle. The blocks themselves are very irregular. For general Stitch 'n Flip instructions, refer to Chapter 1 (page 6). Re-iron the freezer-paper pattern to the top of the pieced muslin, then trim to size. When all the muslin pieces of a section have been Stitch 'n Flipped, join pieces together to complete that section before moving on to another.

4. For C SECTION: Sew C1 to C2 to C3. Sew C4 to C5 to C6. Sew C1-C3 unit to C4-C6 unit.

5. For D SECTION: Sew D1 to D2, add D3 and D4. Sew D5 to D6, add D7 and D8. Sew D1-D4 unit to D5-D8 unit.

6. For E SECTION: Sew E1 to E2, add E3 and E4. Sew E5 to E6. Sew E7 to E8. Sew E1-E4 unit to E5-E6 unit, add E7-E8 unit.

7. For BB SECTION: Sew BB1 to BB2, add BB3. Sew BB4 to BB5 to BB6, add BB7, the add BB8. Sew BB1-BB3 unit to BB4-BB8 unit.

8. For EE section: Sew EE1 to EE2 to EE3. Sew EE4 to EE5, add EE6. Sew EE1-EE3 unit to EE4-EE6 unit.

9. For FF SECTION: Sew FF1 to FF2, add FF3. Sew FF4 to FF5, add FF6. Sew FF1-FF3 unit to FF4-FF6 unit.

10. For GG SECTION: Sew GG1 to GG2, add GG3. Sew GG4 to GG5. Sew GG1-GG3 unit to GG4-GG5 unit.

11. For the TRUNK (T) SECTION: Sew T1 to T2. Sew T3 to T4. Sew T5 to T6, add T7 and T8. Sew T9 to T10 to T11. Sew T12 to T13 to T14 to T15 to T16. Sew T17 to T18 to T19 to T20 to T21 to T22. Sew T17-T22 unit to T5-T8 unit to T1-T2 unit to T9-T11 unit to T3-T4 unit to T12-T16 unit.

12. Continue to sew all section pieces together, including the branches.

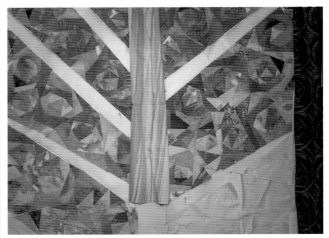

Tree in progress

Quilt Assembly

1. Join all of the left side sections together with the branches in between. Repeat for the right side.

2. Sew the sides of the tree to each side of the trunk.

3. Sew together the border trapezoid pieces, alternating the two pattern sizes, making one long strip.

4. Cut the top and bottom lengths to 47 ½". Stitch to the top and bottom of the quilt. Press.

5. Cut the sides to 78 ½". Stitch to the quilt. Press.

Quilting

I gathered some aspen leaves to get a feel for the shapes I wanted to quilt. I also studied aspen bark. The trunk and branches were quilted with the intention of creating depth within them. I quilted leaves into the border to integrate the tree with the border, using YLI Jeans Stitch thread for emphasis.

Tip *For the binding, use leftover scraps from the border. Cut all the pieces 2 ¼" wide, then stitch them together into one long piece.*

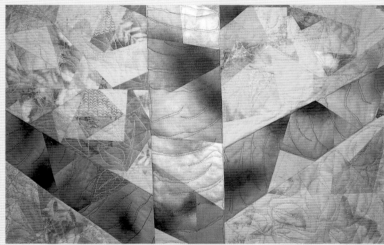

Autumn Aspen *quilting designs*

*Quilting design for leaves
Enlarge to desired size.*

Autumn Aspen Pattern

Enlarge to 47" x 68", or approximately 800%.

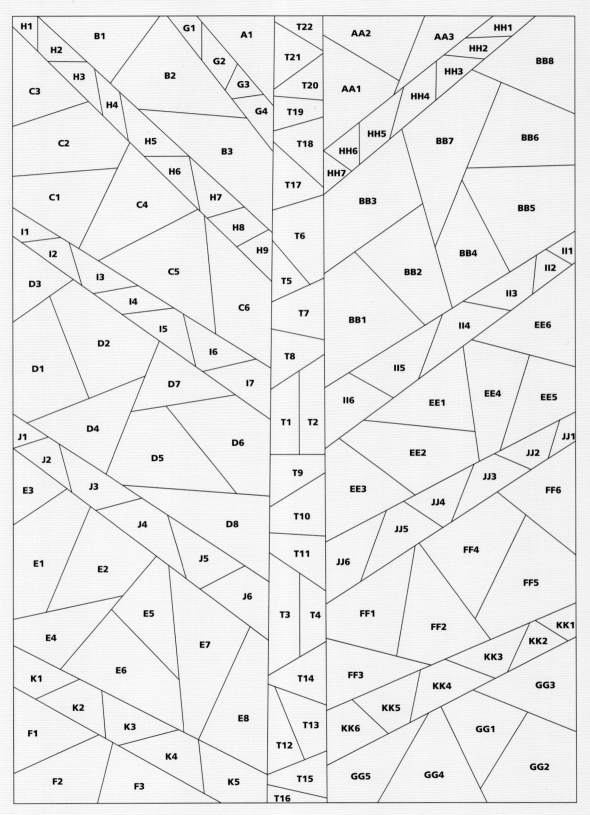

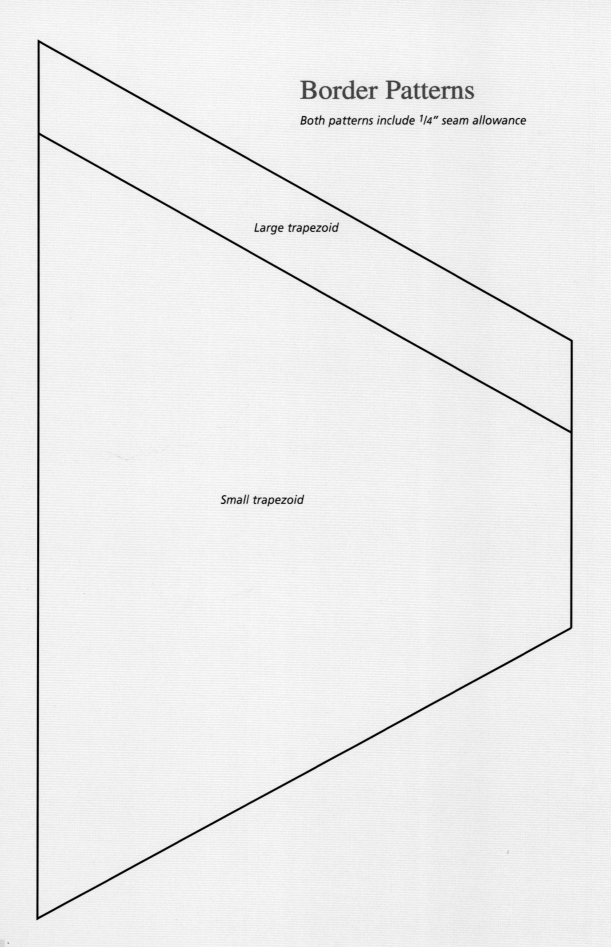

Border Patterns

Both patterns include ¹⁄₄" seam allowance

Large trapezoid

Small trapezoid

Anniversary Bouquet

Anniversary Bouquet by Jean Wells Keenan, 51 ½" x 57 ½", 1999.

P R O J E C T

Anniversary Bouquet

Anniversary Bouquet by Jean Wells Keenan, 51 ½" x 57 ½", 1999.

PROJECT

Designing **from Nature**   57

Jean, who lives in Sisters, Oregon, is an avid gardener. Her garden is filled with a variety of flower types. There is one flower, however, that is almost impossible for her to grow—the rose. The deer just eat them too quickly! When her husband, John, gives her roses for her birthday or anniversary, it's a very special occasion. She dries the petals and puts them in drawers to savor their fragrance. Over the years she has collected pictures of roses so she can study their color and shape. Stitch 'n Flip is the perfect technique for creating rose blocks, and it's a way for Jean to remember the bouquets from John. Once the blocks were made, the challenge was placing them in a still-life setting and creating curves on the outer edges of the petals. After she pieced the rose blocks together, she appliquéd the outer petals so that they better resembled their natural shape.

Fabric Selection

Pink is the first color Jean thinks of when she thinks of roses; however, as she started making the blocks, she found that using only soft pink didn't result in the depth that she desired. She looked through gardening catalogs and found that many pink roses have a melon-like color within their petals. Jean auditioned fabrics in this color group and it instantly perked up the bouquet. The brighter and deeper tones make the quilt "sing." Her composition is a still-life framed within a box. She chose a deeper red shade for the box that makes the bouquet stand out. She used a brown texture fabric for the table and a variety of grays for the tin holding the bouquet.

Color palette

Materials

Muslin: 2 1/4 yards
Wide range of pink values for the roses: 2 yards
Pink-and-yellow print: 1/8 yard
Four different deep reds: 1/3 yard for the background
Green: 1/3 yard for the leaves
Medium greens: 1/8 yard for the background (of a slightly different value from leaf fabric; Jean used scraps)
Dark and medium grays: 1 yard for the container
Light gray: 1/8 yard for the container
Border and binding: 1 1/8 yards of a neutral print to frame the rose bouquet
Backing: 3 yards
Batting: 55" x 61"
Template plastic

Cutting

Muslin: Referring to the drawing of the quilt, cut the muslin foundation for all sections except the borders. Using a pencil, label the cut size for future reference. Lightly pencil circular rose shapes on the appropriate pieces. At the bottom of the quilt, you'll see diagonal lines, which indicate where the table is under the container. Pencil in those lines.

Pinks: Cut one 1"-wide, one 1 1/2"-wide, and one 2"-wide strip. Cut more as needed.

Green: Make templates using the patterns on page 64. Cut three large and five medium leaves.

Border: Cut five 4 1/2"-wide strips and sew them together, end to end. Cut into a 53 1/2" length, a 25 1/2" length, and a 10 1/2" length for the side borders. Then cut into a 51 1/2" length for the top border and a 47 1/2" length for the bottom border. Refer to the quilt assembly diagram.

Block Construction

1. For the roses, start by cutting a square for the center, then trim the edges so it appears round. The construction of this block is very similar to the Johnny-Jump-Up block (page 7). The larger the flower, the larger the center shape needs to be. For some of the roses, Jean used a pink-and-yellow print to mimic roses that have a bit of yellow in the center. For general Stitch 'n Flip instructions, refer to Chapter 1 (page 6).

2. Use narrower strips in the center of the flower and graduate outward to wider strips. As the flower gets larger, you may find it necessary to make additional angle cuts in the strip to keep the flower circular. (Refer to Step 4 in *Moon Phases*, page 42.)

Measurements given in cut sizes

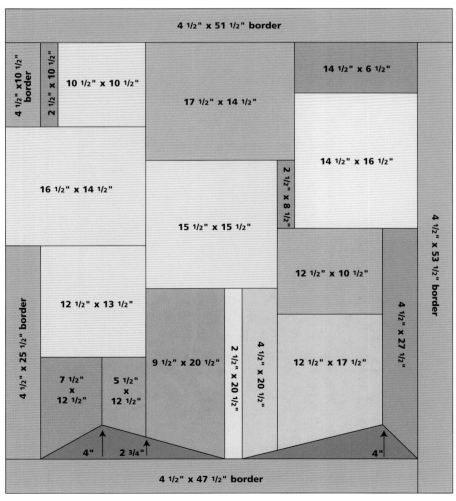

3. When you reach the penciled-in circular rose shape, make sure you end with a 2"-wide strip. Start stitching ¼" in from the raw edge of this strip. These outer edges need to be left unstitched at this time. Eventually they will be trimmed into petal shapes, then hand appliquéd into place after the quilt top is assembled.

Edge of rose to be appliquéd

4. Fold back the last round of petals toward the flower's center. Pin the fabric to keep it out of the way while you piece the background. For the background, use larger wedges of fabric. Refer to the photograph of the quilt for color placement (page 57). Trim the blocks to cut size of muslin keeping last row of petals out of the way.

5. On the left-hand edge, where the rose extends to the border, slip some border fabric under the petals.

6. Use larger wedges of fabric for piecing the container. Refer to the photograph of the quilt (page 57). Use the lightest gray at the narrow corner between the dark side on the left and the medium side on the right. Trim to the cut size of the muslin. Add the table fabric last, at the bottom of the container and to the left.

Quilt Assembly

1. Stitch the blocks together in sections. There will be tight spots where you partially stitch a seam, join another seam, then come back to finish the first seam. Add the left-hand side border as you do the piecing. Then add the bottom border, the right-hand side border, and lastly the top border. Press seams toward the borders.

2. Position the leaves, tucking them under the edges of the rose petals. You may need to trim excess leaf fabric from under the petals. Pin them in place.

3. Remove the pins from the petals and gently cut the curve on the outer edge of the strip to resemble rose petals.

4. Hand appliqué the petals and leaves into place. Refer to page 12 for appliqué instructions.

Quilting

Jean enlarged photographs of roses in a photocopy machine, then traced the petals to achieve the effect of their natural folds. Using an embroidery foot, she started at the center of a rose and stitched around it until she reached the outer edges. For the leaves, Jean zigzagged around the edge first, then quilted the veins. She filled the tin container with long zigzag stitching lines to create texture on its surface. In the background areas, she "echo stitched" the rose petal shapes. Finally, she filled the wood frame border with a simple wood grain design.

Anniversary Bouquet *quilting designs*

Anniversary Bouquet
Quilting Designs

Enlarge to desired size.

Start here

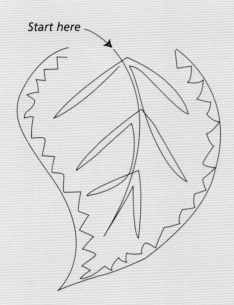

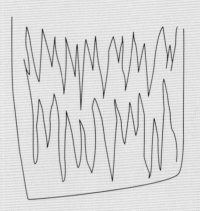

Tip To carry an impression of the rose and leaf into the binding, add matching leaf or rose fabric into the binding. To do this, stitch the quilt binding to within an inch of the leaf or rose. Lay the piece of the leaf or rose binding over the leaf or rose on the quilt top. Fold back a 1/4" seam allowance toward the wrong side of the leaf or rose binding. The folded edge should match the edge of the leaf or rose. Pin in place. Lay the quilt binding on top of the leaf or rose binding section and trim 1/4" beyond the folded edge of it. Pin in place. Complete this process for each side of the leaf and rose. Finish stitching the binding in place. When you turn the binding over the raw edge of the quilt, it will be necessary to hand stitch the two fabrics together where they meet on the binding.

Carry the rose fabric into the binding

Anniversary Bouquet
Leaf Patterns

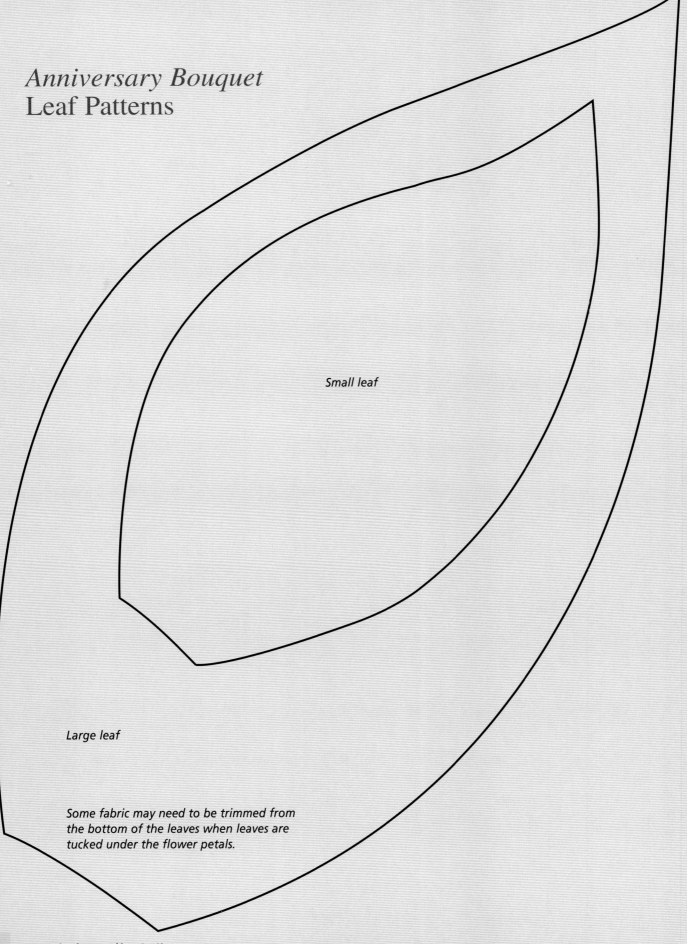

Small leaf

Large leaf

Some fabric may need to be trimmed from
the bottom of the leaves when leaves are
tucked under the flower petals.

Tree Tablerunner

Tree Tablerunner by Mary Ferguson, 17 1/2" x 47 1/2", 1999.

This tablerunner is a great accent to any table. Mary enjoyed making the pillows on page 37 so much that I asked if she would make a tablerunner. I wanted something lively and bright, with a couple of trees and a sun. Mary took the idea and had fun with it.

Fabric Selection

Mary chose light and dark greens for the trees and bright blues for the sky. The sky fabric has bits of white in it, which really adds to the scene. Within the trees, there's a deep brown with a touch of green, suggestive of moss. For the sun, Mary used yellows and then added a small amount of orange as an accent.

Materials

Muslin: 1/2 yard
Greens: 3/4 yard for trees
Yellows: 1/3 yard for sun. (Make sure there is a piece that is at least 7" square.)
Blues: 1/3 yard for sky
Borders and sashing: 1/2 yard blue
Backing and binding: 1 1/2 yards
Batting: 21" x 51"

Cutting

Muslin: Cut two 13 1/2" x 14 1/2" rectangles and one 13 1/2" square.
Greens: Cut into 1"- to 2"-wide strips for piecing.
Blues: Cut into 2"- to 3"-wide strips for piecing.
Yellows: Cut a 7" square from one yellow for the sun. Cut the remaining yellows into 3 1/2"-wide strips.
Sashing: Cut two 1 1/2" x 13 1/2" strips.
Borders:
Cut two 2 1/2" x 17 1/2" strips for the top and bottom. Cut three 2 1/2"-wide strips and piece them together end to end. Then cut into two 43 1/2" lengths for the side borders.

Block Construction

1. The construction of the sun block is very similar to the Johnny-Jump-Up block (page 7); however, the trees start with a triangle. For general Stitch 'n Flip instructions, refer to Chapter 1 (page 6).

2. Using the 13 ½" square of muslin, start with the sun block. From the 7" square of yellow, trim the sides until you have seven or eight edges.

3. Add one round of 3 ½" wide yellow strips.

4. For the next round, after attaching the strip, trim the strip into a triangle for a sun point.

5. Create more points on the sun by piecing together a little of the yellow and blue fabric, making a strip to stitch onto the sun block. To do this, cut a triangle from the yellow fabric. With a blue strip partially under the yellow triangle, cut the angle of the yellow triangle on the blue strip. Stitch the yellow triangle to the blue strip. Repeat this process on the other side of the triangle. This creates a strip with blue on the sides of the yellow triangle.

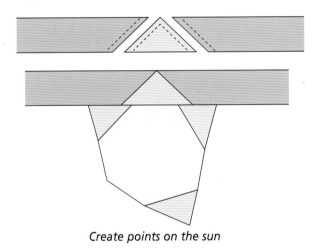

Create points on the sun

6. Add this strip to the sun block.

7. You will need two to four of these strips to have eight points on your sun.

8. Once you have added the points, fill the rest of the muslin with blue. Press. Trim to 13 ½" square.

9. For the trees, start with a triangle and add strips to the sides until you reach your desired size. Remember that the shape of your beginning triangle will determine the shape of your tree.

10. Once you have a finished tree, add blue strips to fill the rest of the muslin.

11. Press. Trim the block to 13 ½" x 14 ½".

Tablerunner Assembly

1. Stitch the 1 ½" x 13 ½" sashing strips to opposite sides of the sun block. Press seams toward the sashing.

2. Add the tree blocks to opposite ends of the sun/sashing unit. Press seams toward the sashing.

3. Stitch the 2 ½" x 43 ½" border strips to the sides of table runner. Press seams toward the border.

4. Stitch the 2 ½" x 17 ½" border strips to the top and bottom of the table runner. Press seams toward the border.

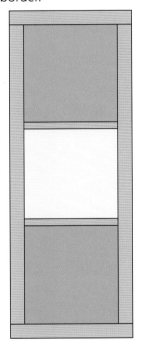

Quilting

Mary used a quilting design that would suggest branches in the trees and clouds in the sky. She quilted a spiral in the center of the sun and echoed its points. Two wavy lines in the border add a decorative curve.

Traditional
Transformations

J ean's idea for the *Magic Carpet* setting was inspired by an antique quilt she once saw in a book. She liked the large triangle shapes and thought that they would be perfect subjects for some interesting piecing. With the Stitch 'n Flip technique, Jean was able to create her desired wedge shapes. The challenge was to make the piecing within the large triangles small enough to create intricate jewel-like shapes.

Magic Carpet

Magic Carpet by Jean Wells Keenan, 80 ½" x 95 ½", 1999.

Fabric Selection

Jean's palette contains rich rusts, greens, browns, golds, and black. She used gold sparingly as an accent. The black sashing defines the triangular shapes as well as the quilt design. Once the blocks were completed, she auditioned border fabrics and decided to use a 1"-wide piece of rusty orange surrounded by a wider piece of black.

Materials

Muslin: 2 2/3 yards
Blocks: 6 yards total of a wide variety of fabrics
Black: 4 2/3 yards for sashing, outer border, and binding
Rusty orange: 1/2 yard for the corner posts and inner border
Backing: 6 1/2 yards
Batting: 84" x 99"
Template plastic

Cutting

Muslin: Cut twenty 13" squares. Cut across the squares diagonally in both directions. This creates 80 triangles.

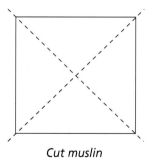

Cut muslin

Blocks: From each of the fabrics for the blocks, cut two 2"-wide strips, except for the accent color; cut it 1 3/4" wide. Cut more strips as needed.
Diagonal sashing: Cut twenty 1 1/2" x 42" strips. Using the template pattern on page 72, cut 80 diagonal sashing pieces.

Sashing: Cut eighteen 2 1/2"-wide strips for the sashing around the blocks. Stitch into one long length. Cut into the following lengths:
Cut fifteen 13 1/2" strips for the vertical sashing between the blocks.
Cut six 58 1/2" lengths for the horizontal sashing.
Cut two 77 1/2" lengths for the side sashing.
Outer border: Cut eight 8 1/2"-wide strips. Stitch strips together end to end. Cut into two 64 1/2" lengths for the top and bottom borders and two 95 1/2" lengths for the side borders.
Inner border: Cut eight 1 1/2"-wide strips. Stitch strips together end to end. Cut into two 62 1/2" lengths for the top and bottom borders and two 79 1/2" lengths for the side borders.
Corner posts: Cut one 1 1/2"-wide strip, then cut into twenty 1 1/2" squares.

Block Construction

1. The Stitch 'n Flip piecing process for *Magic Carpet* follows a triangular shape to echo the triangular shape of the foundation. Cut a triangle and place it near the center of the muslin. It's more interesting if the triangles are not all alike. Pin the triangle near the middle of the foundation. For general Stitch 'n Flip instructions, refer to Chapter 1 (page 6).

Start the block

2. Place the next strip onto one of the sides, right sides together. Stitch and flip. Trim the strip to form a triangle. You'll find that the width of the strip and the length of the previous seam determine the shape of the triangle. This is what makes the piecing visually interesting. Press.

Add to the triangle

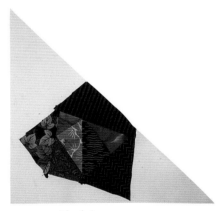

Block in progress

3. Continue covering the foundation. Press. Place the triangle template on the pieced triangle and trim around the edges. Make 80 triangles.

Finished section

4. Stitch a diagonal sashing strip between a pair of triangles. Press the seam toward the sashing strip. Make 40 pairs of triangles.

5. Stitch a corner post between two diagonal sashing strips. Press toward the sashing. Stitch this strip between the pairs of triangles. Press toward the sashing. Make 20 blocks. Trim to 13 ¹/₂".

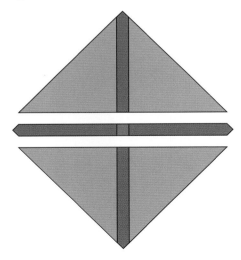

Add diagonal sashing strips

Quilt Assembly

1. Arrange the blocks as shown. Stitch the 13 ½" vertical sashing strips between the blocks. Press toward the sashing. Add the horizontal sashing. Press toward the sashing. Add the side sashing. Press toward the sashing.

2. Add the inner accent top and bottom borders, then the inner side borders. Press seams toward the border.

3. Add the outer side borders, then the outer top and bottom borders. Press seams toward the outer border.

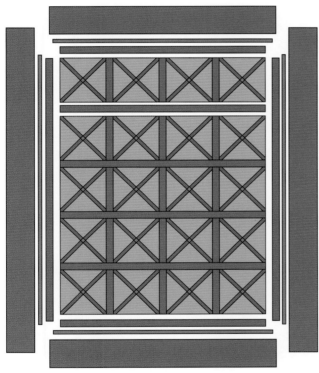

Quilt assembly

Quilting

For the quilting, Jean echoed the triangular shapes, much like gridwork.

Magic Carpet quilting designs

Magic Carpet Patterns

Both patterns include ¹/4" seam allowance

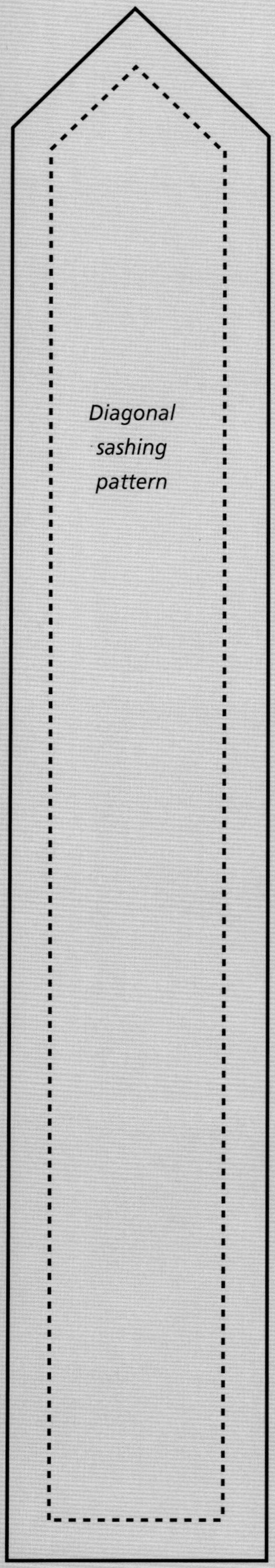

Diagonal
sashing
pattern

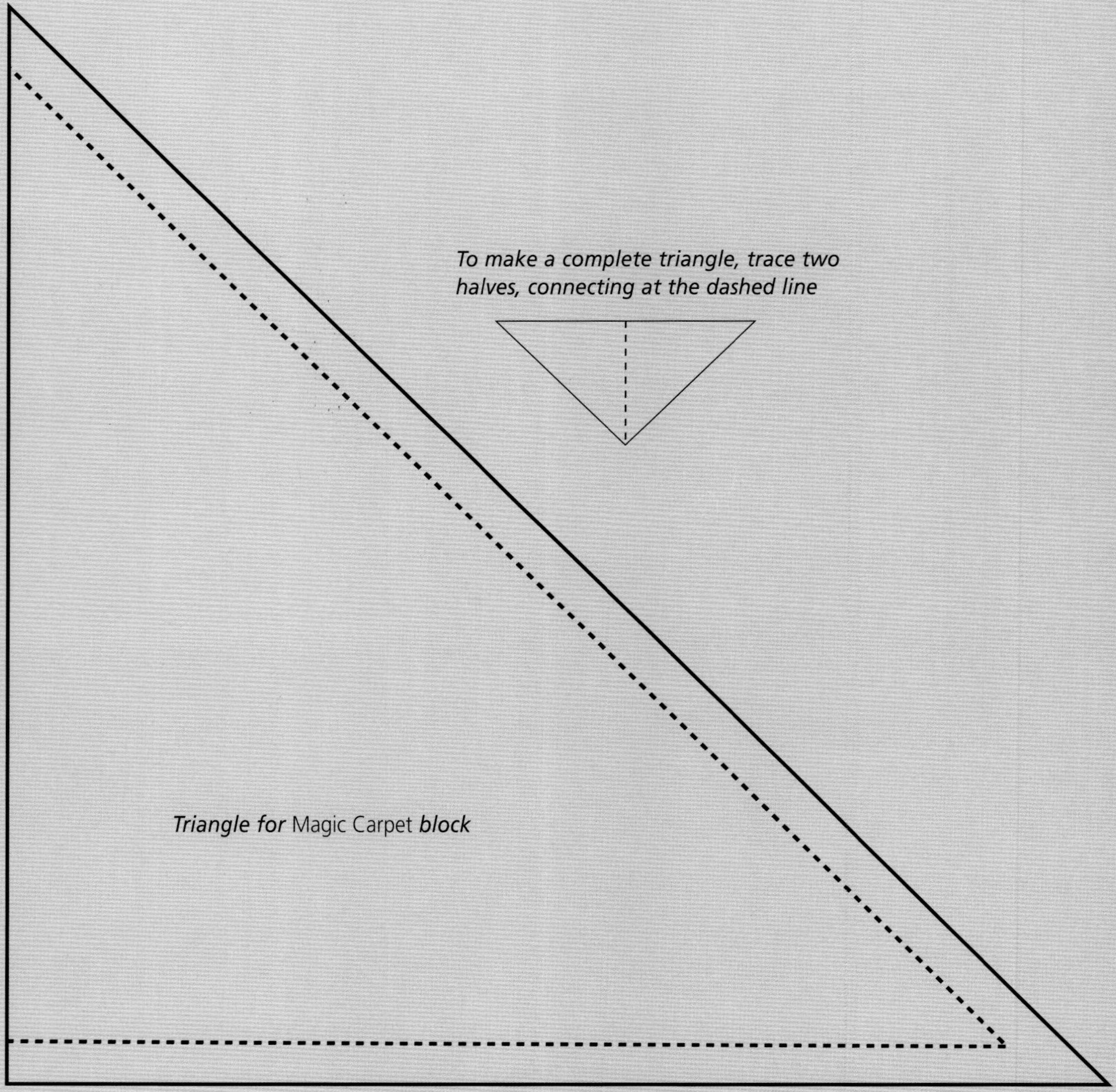

To make a complete triangle, trace two
halves, connecting at the dashed line

Triangle for Magic Carpet *block*

Vintage Fans

Vintage Fans by Barbara Ferguson, 33" x 33", 1999.

*V*intage Fans uses the traditional pieced fan block and adapts it to the Stitch 'n Flip technique. The fan pieces are randomly shaped, which gives it an old-fashioned feel. Barbara auditioned several settings before deciding on this one. The other settings are shown on page 77. This idea could be easily translated to a larger quilt. This size works nicely as a table centerpiece, chair throw, or wallhanging.

Fabric Selection

Regardless of the palette you choose, you must pay attention to contrast in order for the quilt to show off the fans. Barbara loves vintage textiles, so I wasn't surprised when she chose this palette. The first step is sorting the fabrics from medium-light to dark values. The darks and medium-darks are set aside for the fans, the medium-lights for the background, the medium green for the base, and the red for the sashing. Take a close look at the fans and you'll see that she occasionally added a surprise medium value, different from the base of the fan. Many of the fabrics used (all of which are prints) are low-contrast and textured.

Fabric palette

Materials

Muslin: 5/8 yard
Variety of darks and medium-darks: 1 1/4 yards total for fans
Medium: 1/4 yard for base
Variety of medium-lights: 1 yard for background
Sashing and inner border: 3/8 yard
Outer border, binding, and backing: 1 2/3 yards
Batting: 37" x 37"
Template plastic

Cutting

Muslin: Cut sixteen 6 1/2" squares.
Fans: Cut 1 1/2"-wide strips from the darks and medium-darks.
Background: Cut 2"-wide strips from the medium-lights.
Base: Cut sixteen bases from the medium, using the template pattern on page 78.
Sashing: Cut two 1" x 12 1/2" strips for the sides, and two 1" x 13 1/2" strips for the top and bottom. Cut four sashing bars 1 1/2" x 6 1/2" each for outer row of blocks.
Inner border: Cut two 1 1/2" x 25 1/2" strips for the sides and two 1 1/2" x 27 1/2" strips for the top and bottom.
Outer border: Cut two 3 1/4" x 27 1/2" strips for the sides and two 3 1/4" x 33" strips for the top and bottom.

Block Construction

1. Your beginning shape is a rectangular strip. For general Stitch 'n Flip instructions, refer to Chapter 1 (page 6).

2. To begin, gently pencil in a fan shape on the muslin. As you can see from Barbara's blocks, they are not all the same. Decide on the first strip and place it in the center of the block, extending at least 1/4" above the pencil line.

Begin the fan shape

3. Place the second strip, right sides together, on top of the first, angling it slightly toward the base. Stitch. Trim excess fabric. Add strips in this manner, creating wedge-like shapes from side to side until the fan shape is filled.

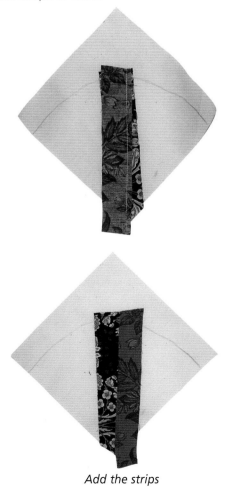

Add the strips

Fan shape

4. To add the background, start with one of your medium-light fabrics. Place it along the top edge of the fan wedges. You will be able to cover about four fans. Stitch in place. Flip and finger-press to the right side without trimming. Place a second strip, covering another four fan wedges. Stitch. Trim the excess fabric from the first strip. Continue until you have covered the ends of all the wedges. Fill in the remainder of the background. Press and square up the block to 6 ½".

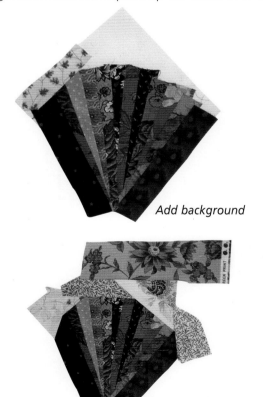

Add background

Fan block

5. Pin the base of the fan in place and hand appliqué. Refer to Chapter 1 (page 12) for instructions. Barbara doesn't trim the excess fan fabric or muslin under the base of the fan. She feels that this gives the base a uniform thickness, in contrast with the rest of the block.

Add the base of the fan

Quilt Assembly

1. Arrange the blocks and sashing strips for the quilt.

2. Stitch the four center blocks together and add the 1" x 12 ½" side sashings, then add the 1" x 13 ½" top and bottom sashings. Press seams toward the sashing.

3. Stitch the four 1 ½" x 6 ½" sashing bars between the outer pairs of blocks as shown. Press seams toward the sashing bars.

4. Add the side block units to the quilt. Press seams toward the sashing.

5. Stitch remaining blocks to each end of the top and bottom block units. Add to the top and bottom of the quilt. Press seams toward the sashing.

6. Add the inner side borders first, then the top and bottom borders. Press seams toward the border. Repeat for the outer borders.

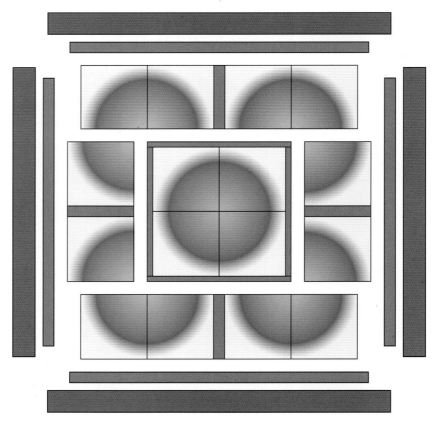

Quilt assembly

Quilting

Vintage Fans has a simple, continuous vine-and-leaf design quilted in the border. The design is narrower for the inner border and wider for the outer border. The variegated thread picks up the colors in the pieced fans. Long, loop-like lines travel through the fan wedges with meandering stippling on the base of the fan.

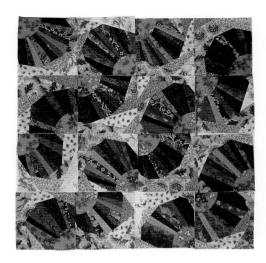

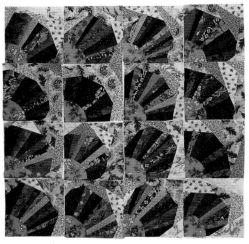

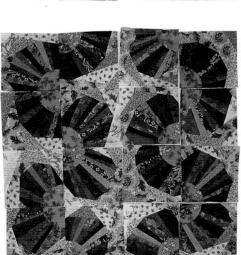

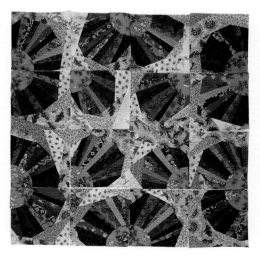

Variations for arranging the blocks

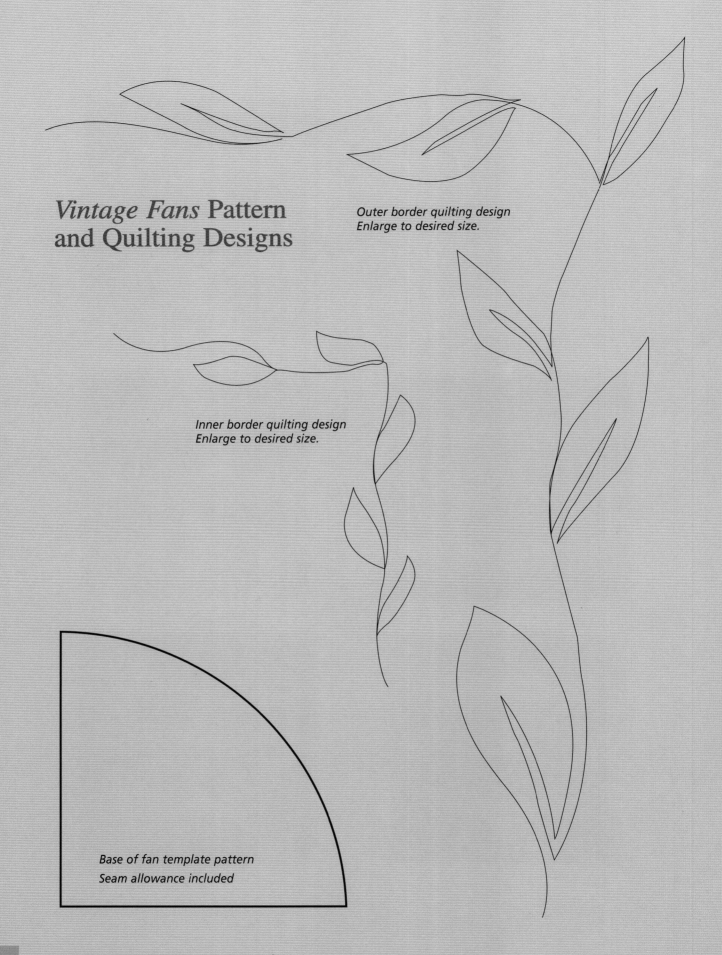

Vintage Fans Pattern and Quilting Designs

Outer border quilting design
Enlarge to desired size.

Inner border quilting design
Enlarge to desired size.

Base of fan template pattern
Seam allowance included

A collection of reproduction textiles creates an old-fashioned mood in *Vintage Fans* by Barbara Ferguson.

Vintage Fan Pillow

Vintage Fan Pillow by Barbara Ferguson, 8" x 8", 1999.

Barbara had one fan block left over, and thought a pillow would be a quick and easy additional project. The pillow block is constructed the same way as the quilt blocks, then bordered with a 1"-wide finished strip (cut 1 1/2" wide). Cut the backing 8 1/2" square. Place the pillow block and backing right sides together and stitch around three sides, leaving one end open for stuffing. Trim the excess fabric from the corners and turn to the right side. Press. Fill with stuffing and stitch the opening closed. Quilting is optional. This pillow makes a great accent piece on a sofa or can be used as a pincushion next to your sewing machine.

Forever in
Blue Jeans

Forever in Blue Jeans by Lawry Thorn, 45 $^3/_4$" x 45 $^3/_4$", 1999.

The song *"Forever in Blue Jeans"* by Neil Diamond was the inspiration for this scrap-style star quilt made in shades of blue. Lawry used the traditional 54-40 or Fight star block and pieced all of the areas with the Stitch 'n Flip technique. The subtle lines from the fabric transitions create a textured effect.

Fabric Selection

Start by pulling together a collection of blues—the more the better. Separate them into light, medium, and dark piles. Make sure you have enough variety to create the mellow blue mood that Lawry achieved.

Materials

Muslin: 2 yards
Light blues: 1 yard
Medium blues: 3/4 yard
Dark blues: 1 yard
Inner border: 1/4 yard
Outer border and binding: 1 1/4 yards
Backing: 2 yards
Batting: 50" x 50"
Template plastic

Cutting

Muslin: Cut nine 4 1/2" squares for "D." The remaining fabric will be cut into rectangles approximately 10" x 22". About 12 rectangles are needed.
Blues: Cut 1 1/4"- and 1 3/4"-wide strips.
Inner border: Cut five 7/8"-wide strips. Stitch together into one long piece. Cut into four 49" lengths.
Outer border: Cut five 4 3/4"-wide strips. Stitch together into one long piece. Cut into four 49" lengths.

Block Construction

1. Strips of fabric stitched together form the Stitch 'n Flip pattern in this quilt design. Begin with a strip rather than a cut shape. For general Stitch 'n Flip instructions, refer to Chapter 1 (page 6).

2. Using one of the 10" x 22" muslin foundations, stitch and flip the light blue strips to it. Vary the width of the strips to create interesting blocks. Repeat this process with medium blues and then dark blues. This gives you Stitch 'n Flip fabric to work with for piecing. Press.

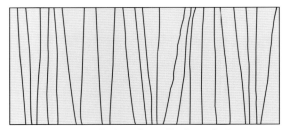

Drawing of pieced muslin foundation

3. Using template plastic, make templates for A, B, and C with the patterns on page 86. Label the templates.

4. Start with the dark blue Stitch 'n Flip fabric. Place template C on top of it. Notice how you can move the template around to make the strip placement more interesting. Cut around the edges. You will need a total of 36 C's. Using template A on the dark blue, cut 36 A's. You may need to make another piece of Stitch 'n Flip fabric to cut all of the A and C pieces.

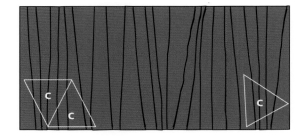

Tip *Lawry likes to use the Tri Tool™ and Recs Tool™, designed by Darlene Zimmerman and Joy Hoffman, for cutting the star angle of the 54-40 or Fight block. The nice thing about the rulers is that the pointed ends are squared off, so once the pieces are cut, they match up exactly before stitching.*

5. Using template B, cut 36 B's from the light blue Stitch 'n Flip fabric. Remember, there is a left side and a right side, so reverse (mirror-image) template B and cut 36 additional reversed B's.

6. Using template A, cut 36 A's using the medium blue Stitch 'n Flip fabric.

7. For D, start with a lopsided square cut from the end of a light strip and place it in the center of the 4 1/2" muslin square. Stitch 'n Flip as described in Chapter 1 (page 6). This resembles the Log Cabin piecing process. Press. Trim to 4 1/2" square.

Make center squares

8. To assemble the nine blocks, choose a dark and a medium of the A shape. Place right sides together and stitch along the diagonal edge. Press the seam open. Make 36 units.

9. Place B on C as shown. Stitch the seam. Press open. Add the reversed B to the other side of C. Press open. Make 36 units.

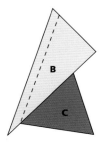

10. Stitch the units together in rows. For the first and third rows, press the seams toward the outside of the block. For the second row, press toward the inside of the block. When Row 1 is joined to Row 2, and so forth, the seams will nest together. Blocks should measure 12 1/2" square.

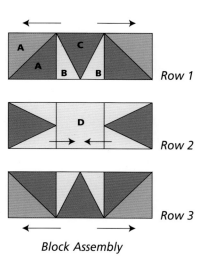

Block Assembly

Quilt Assembly

1. This quilt has mitered border corners. Stitch an inner and outer border strip together. Repeat three more times. Press seam allowance toward the outer border.

Quilt assembly

2. Fold the border strip in half and mark it with a pin. Pin it to the center of one of the sides of the quilt. Pin it to the corners, leaving a pin 1/4" from the raw edge. There will be excess border fabric extending beyond the raw edge. Stitch from pin to pin. Repeat on the other three sides of the quilt. Press the seam allowance toward the border.

3. Lay the quilt on the ironing board, wrong side up. Lay the top border over the side border. Fold back the top border, creating a 45° angle, and press the fold. You can use a square ruler to check the angle.

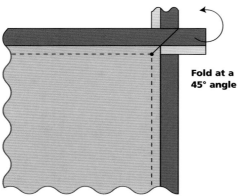

Fold at a 45° angle

4. Pin the two borders right sides together. Beginning at the inside corner of the quilt, stitch on the fold line to the outer edge. Trim excess fabric to 1/4" and press seam open. Repeat for the other three corners.

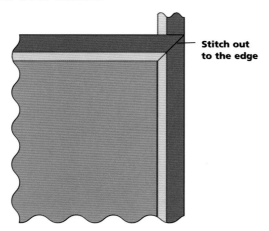

Stitch out to the edge

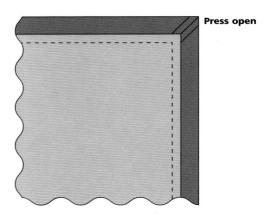

Press open

Quilting

Lawry used a spiral-like overall quilting pattern, matching the threads to the different areas of color.

Forever in Blue Jeans *quilting designs*

The icy blue palette of *Forever in Blue Jeans* by Lawry Thorn is reminiscent of winter in central Oregon.

Forever in Blue Jeans Patterns

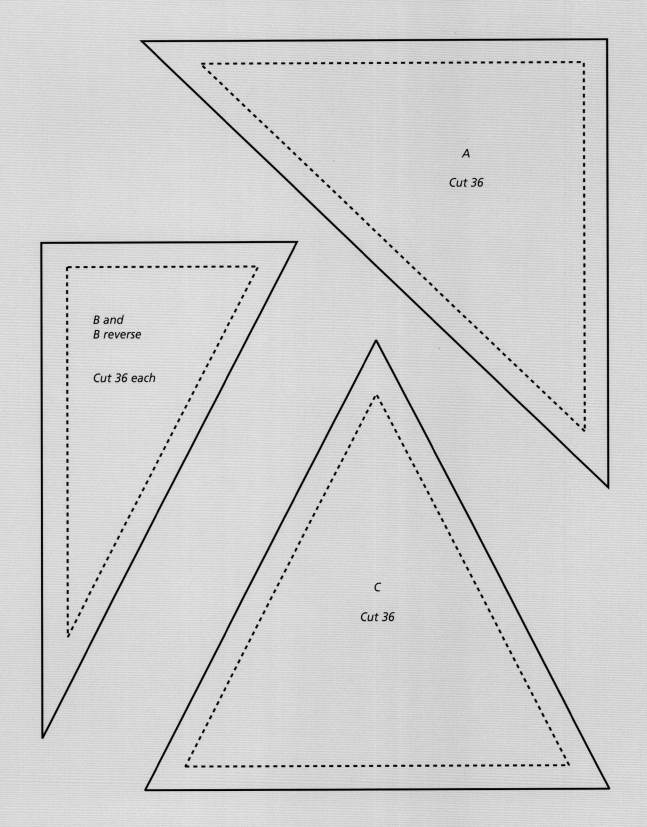

A

Cut 36

B and
B reverse

Cut 36 each

C

Cut 36

A Quilter's
Journey

Cathedral Falls on the Metolius River

When I asked Barb to make a quilt for this book, I knew that she would create something beautiful. The story behind the creation of *Cathedral Falls* is a journey through Barb's design process, which uses Stitch 'n Flip as the piecing method. I included her quilt and design notes as the last chapter with the hope of inspiring you to take your design ideas to another level—to make your own works of art inspired by special places, photographs, and your imagination. Following are Barb's notes from her design process.

Cathedral Falls

Cathedral Falls by Barb Tate, 31" x 43", 1999.

Notes from Barb

I first saw Cathedral Falls in August, 1998. It is a series of springs that literally pour out of a hillside into the Metolius River in central Oregon. What captured my attention was the amazing color of the water—a translucent turquoise that appeared to be lit from the bottom of the riverbed. When Valori asked me to do a quilt for her book, I knew immediately that I wanted to capture the setting of Cathedral Falls in a quilt.

Valori and I spent an afternoon on the riverbank, watching and photographing the shifting colors that occurred as the sun cleared the surrounding trees and hills. The silvery spray falling from the hillside into the river was an appropriate counterpoint to the white of the falls. Shades of green in the falls and the forest above ranged from deep forest to yellow-green. The rocks in the riverbed varied from brown to green, depending on the amount of moss growing on them and the lighting. Throughout the afternoon the colors shifted within a matter of minutes.

The Stitch 'n Flip technique simplified translating what I saw (and was fascinated by) into a wall-hanging. First, I broke down the various parts of the picture—actually a composite of three different photographs—into manageable pieces or strips of varying widths.

Next, I broke down the widths into units. I found that cutting the units at an angle made the completed strip more visually interesting. With the Stitch 'n Flip technique, I was actually painting with fabric, adding light and definition to specific areas as I created the units. I focused on one section of an area before moving onto the next.

Composition of photography

Simplified drawings of the photographs creating sections for piecing

Beginning the piecing

I started with the bark of the fallen Ponderosa tree and quickly discovered that the process was easier to handle by working with smaller units. Using strips for the forest made working in that area manageable.

As I progressed to the falls, I used tracing paper to make the needed odd-shaped units. I cut out the muslin foundation pieces based on the tracing paper "templates."

Tracing of the falls

The key was to keep my design simple enough to piece later. In some areas I succeeded better than others.

The forest

The completed falls

Detail of the falls

Originally, I thought of using one piece of hand-painted fabric for the water and quilting it to create movement. However, by the time I had finished the forest and the falls, I knew that one piece of fabric wouldn't feel right; it would be too static for the pieced areas around it. I decided to use various pieces for the water, which did work.

Cathedral Falls *before being pieced together*

Sewing all of the various units or strips together was like working a puzzle; it took concentration. Within the water section, there were some areas that required using a chalk wheel to create sewing lines so that the pieces would fit together.

Squaring up the piece was another challenge. I ended up hanging the finished top on my design wall and suspending weighted strings from the top of it. The strings gave me straight lines to work from and were invaluable to the squaring-up process.

The final step, the quilting of *Cathedral Falls*, was the icing on the cake. Using my photos as a guide, I quilted what I saw: leaves, pine needles, waterfalls, rocks, and bark. Since I am not particularly adept at drawing, quilting these motifs was challenging. Because the wallhanging was so heavily quilted, a final squaring up was required. This time, it was much easier to do using rulers and mats.

The Stitch 'n Flip technique was perfect for achieving the visual effect that I desired—a vivid impression of Cathedral Falls. It provided freedom to play with color and light in a way that I hadn't experienced before.

Cathedral Falls *quilting designs*

Conclusion

Congratulations! You have completed your first Stitch 'n Flip project! I hope you are happy with your creation and excited about this fun and easy technique. Stitch 'n Flip will open up a world of creativity and spark endless quilting design possibilities.

Sources

If you are interested in any of the products mentioned in this book, check with your local quilt shop. If you're unable to find them, contact The Stitchin' Post. Also, The Stitchin' Post is equipped to transfer photographs onto fabric.

The Stitchin' Post
P.O. Box 280
Sisters, OR 07759
(541) 549-6061
e-mail: stitchin@empnet.com
http:/www.stitchinpost.com

Quilters Dream Cotton Batting
Kelsun, Inc.
3205 Foxgrove Lane
Chesapeake, VA 23321
888-COTTON-4

Tri Tool and Recs Tool
Quilt House
95 Mayhill Street
Saddle Brook, NJ 07663

YLI Jeans Stitch Thread
YLI Corporation
Rock Hill, SC

Fabrico Dual Markers
Tsukinek, Inc.
15411 NE 95th Street
Redmond, WA 98052

Synthrapol
Craft Industries Limited
Somerset, MA 02726-0038

For quilting supplies:
Cotton Patch Mail Order
3405 Brown Avenue, Dept. CTB
Lafayette, CA 94549
e-mail: quiltusa@yahoo.com
http://www.quiltusa.com
(800) 835-4418
(925) 283-7883

Recommended Reading

Start Quilting with Alex Anderson
by Alex Anderson
(C&T Publishing)

The Photo Transfer Handbook
by Jean Ray Laury
(C&T Publishing)

Quilting Your Memories
by Sandy Bonsib
(That Patchwork Place/Martingale and Company)

Machine Quilting Made Easy
by Maurine Noble
(That Patchwork Place/Martingale and Company)

Index

Bold indicates a quilt or project name

About the Author

Photography is the heart of all of Valori's creative endeavors and plays an important role in her quilt inspiration and designs. She is a graduate of Pacific Northwest College of Art and received the "Outstanding Photographer of the Year" award in 1997. Valori and her mother, Jean Wells, have collaborated on two previous books, *Everything Flowers* and *Through the Garden Gate*. Valori has designed three lines of fabric and is working on future lines for Quilters Only. She lives in Sisters, Oregon.

Other Fine Books from C&T Publishing

Appliqué 12 Easy Ways! : Charming Quilts, Giftable Projects & Timeless Techniques, Elly Sienkiewicz

The Art of Classic Quiltmaking, Harriet Hargrave and Sharyn Craig

The Best of Baltimore Beauties, Elly Sienkiewicz

Civil War Women: Their Quilts: Their Roles: Activities for Re-Enactors, Barbara Brackman

Color From the Heart: Seven Great Ways to Make Quilts with Colors You Love, Gai Perry

Color Play: Easy Steps for Imaginative Colors in Quilts, Joen Wolfrom

Crazy with Cotton, Diana Leone

Curves in Motion: Quilt Designs & Techniques, Judy B. Dales

Deidre Scherer: Work in Fabric & Thread, Deidre Scherer

Designing the Doll: From Concept to Construction, Susanna Oroyan

Diane Phalen Quilts: 10 Projects to Celebrate the Season, Diane Phalen

Exploring Machine Trapunto: New Dimensions, Hari Walner

Fabric Shopping with Alex Anderson, Seven Projects to Help You: Make Successful Choices, Build Your Confidence, Add to Your Fabric Stash, Alex Anderson

Fancy Appliqué: 12 Lessons to Enhance Your Skills, Elly Sienkiewicz

Fantastic Fabric Folding: Innovative Quilting Projects, Rebecca Wat

Floral Stitches: An Illustrated Stitch Guide, Judith Baker Montano

Focus on Features: Life-like Portrayals in Appliqué, Charlotte Warr Andersen

Freddy's House: Brilliant Color in Quilts, Freddy Moran

Free Stuff for Collectors on the Internet, Judy Heim and Gloria Hansen

Free Stuff for Crafty Kids on the Internet, Judy Heim and Gloria Hansen

Free Stuff for Doll Lovers on the Internet, Judy Heim and Gloria Hansen

Free Stuff for Gardeners on the Internet, Judy Heim and Gloria Hansen

Free Stuff for Home Décor on the Internet, Judy Heim and Gloria Hansen

Free Stuff for Quilters on the Internet, 2nd Ed. Judy Heim and Gloria Hansen

Free Stuff for Sewing Fanatics on the Internet, Judy Heim and Gloria Hansen

Free Stuff for Stitchers on the Internet, Judy Heim and Gloria Hansen

Free-Style Quilts: A "No Rules" Approach, Susan Carlson

Hand Quilting with Alex Anderson: Six Projects for Hand Quilters, Alex Anderson

Heirloom Machine Quilting, Third Edition, Harriet Hargrave

Jacobean Rhapsodies: Composing with 28 Appliqué Designs, Patricia B. Campbell and Mimi Ayars

Kaleidoscopes : Wonders of Wonder, Cozy Baker

Kaleidoscopes & Quilts, Paula Nadelstern

Make Any Block Any Size, Joen Wolfrom

Mariner's Compass Quilts, New Directions, Judy Mathieson

Mastering Quilt Marking: Marking Tools & Techniques, Choosing Stencils, Matching Borders & Corners, Pepper Cory

Michael James: Art & Inspirations, Michael James

The New England Quilt Museum Quilts: Featuring the Story of the Mill Girls, With Instructions for 5 Heirloom Quilts, Jennifer Gilbert

On the Surface: Thread Embellishment & Fabric Manipulation, Wendy Hill

Pieced Flowers, Ruth B. McDowell

Pieced Roman Shades: Turn Your Favorite Quilt Patterns into Window Hangings, Terrell Sundermann

Piecing: Expanding the Basics, Ruth B. McDowell

Quilt It for Kids: 11 Projects, Sports, Fantasy & Animal Themes, Quilts for Children of All Ages, Pam Bono

The Quilted Garden: Design & Make Nature-Inspired Quilts, Jane Sassaman

Quilting with the Muppets, The Jim Henson Company in Association with Children's Television Workshop

Quilts from Europe, Projects and Inspiration, Gül Laporte

Rx for Quilters: Stitcher-Friendly Advice for Every Body, Susan Delaney Mech, M.D.

Say It with Quilts, Diana McClun and Laura Nownes

Scrap Quilts: The Art of Making Do, Roberta Horton

Shadow Quilts: Easy-to-Design Multiple Image Quilts, Patricia Magaret and Donna Slusser

Six Color World: Color, Cloth, Quilts & Wearables, Yvonne Porcella

Skydyes: A Visual Guide to Fabric Painting, Mickey Lawler

Small Scale Quiltmaking: Precision, Proportion, and Detail, Sally Collins

Smashing Sets: Excititng Ways to Arrange Quilt Blocks, Margaret J. Miller

Special Delivery Quilts, Patrick Lose

Stripes in Quilts, Mary Mashuta

A Thimbleberries Housewarming, Lynette Jensen

Tradition with a Twist: Variations on Your Favorite Quilts, Blanche Young and Dalene Young Stone

Travels with Peaky and Spike: Doreen Speckmann's Quilting Adventures, Doreen Speckmann

Wild Birds: Designs for Appliqué & Quilting, Carol Armstrong

Willowood: Further Adventures in Buttonhole Stitch Appliqué, Jean Wells

Women of Taste: A Collaboration Celebrating Quilt Artists and Chefs, Girls, Inc.

Other favorites by Valori Wells from C&T Publishing, Inc.:

Through the Garden Gate
Quilters and Their Gardens
by Jean & Valori Wells

Everything Flowers
Quilts from the Garden
by Jean & Valori Wells

For more information write for a free catalog:
C&T Publishing, Inc.
P.O. Box 1456
Lafayette, CA 94549
(800) 284-1114
e-mail: ctinfo@ctpub.com
http://www.ctpub.com